Gatheringplaces

Balinese Architecture — A Spiritual & Spatial Orientation

Published by Times Editions—Marshall Cavendish
An imprint of Marshall Cavendish International
1 New Industrial Road, Singapore 536196

Other Marshall Cavendish Offices:
Marshall Cavendish Ltd. 119 Wardour Street, London W1F OUW, UK • Marshall Cavendish
Corporation. 99 White Plains Road, Tarrytown NY 10591-9001, USA • Marshall Cavendish
Beijing. D31A, Huatingjiayuan, No. 6, Beisihuanzhonglu, Chaoyang District, Beijing,
The People's Republic of China, 100029 • Marshall Cavendish International (Thailand) Co Ltd.
253 Asoke, 12th Flr, Sukhumvit 21 Road, Klongtoey Nua, Wattana, Bangkok 10110, Thailand
• Marshall Cavendish (Malaysia) Sdn Bhd, Times Subang, Lot 46, Subang Hi-Tech Industrial
Park, Batu Tiga, 40000 Shah Alam, Selangor Darul Ehsan, Malaysia

Marshall Cavendish is a trademark of Times Publishing Limited

National Library Board Singapore Cataloguing in Publication Data
Walker, Barbara.
Gathering places : Balinese architecture — a spiritual & spatial
orientation / Barbara Walker, Jay Graham.
– Singapore : Times Editions-Marshall Cavendish, c2005.
p. cm.
ISBN : 981-232-918-8
1. Religious architecture – Indonesia – Bali Island. 2. Public architecture
– Indonesia – Bali Island. 3. Ethnic architecture – Indonesia – Bali Island.
4. Landscape architecture – Indonesia – Bali Island.
I. Graham, Jay. II. Title.
NA1526.6.B34
720.95986 — dc21   SLS2005034139

Printed in Singapore by Times Graphics Pte Ltd

Barbara Walker • Jay Graham

Gathering
places
Balinese Architecture — A Spiritual & Spatial Orientation

mc **Times Editions**
Marshall Cavendish

For Susan and Mark who have
given unconditional love and support
to their nomad Mother

Contents

Acknowledgements

Thank you to the Balinese people—you have provided the inspiration for this work.

I am grateful to the people of my adopted village Penestanan and others in the nearby villages of Ubud who freely gave of their time and so willingly shared their knowledge of the Balinese culture. They would frequently drop by Pak Rasman's bamboo *lumbung*, my rice field home, to just say hello and to sit a bit. The verandah became a 'gathering place', a place to *omong-omong*, to talk and be together.

My daughter Susan wrote after a visit to Bali: "When I think of my time in Bali, I picture a rainy afternoon on your open white-tiled porch, colourful cushions thrown here and there with you and your friends sitting and talking, drinking rich dark Bali *kopi*, smoking Indonesian clove cigarettes and sharing time together. It is the thing I remember the very most about Bali, that gathering together, just enjoying each other's company without an agenda or a plan, a goal or a reason... in the United States we call it 'hangin' out'. We're not really good at it... we always have to go somewhere and do something, dinner out, a movie, a hike, something. Balinese are the experts at just 'hangin out', they really are completely comfortable just being together."

It was during those hours of conversation on the verandah discussing the Balinese culture that the idea for *Gathering Places* came about.

Thank you, I. Made Suata for your philosophical ideas of *adat*, *budaya* and *agama*. To I. Gede Wiyartha for your drawings and sketches for the Architectural Notebook. To Ketut Karta, who for many years helped me to experience the beautiful traditions of Bali. To Wayan Muklin, cook extraordinaire, who taught me much.

Thank you, dear friends Sheila Haisfield and Richard Leavitt who patiently listened, encouraged, searched for sites and sometimes generously provided room, board and *gudang* space.

Jay Graham and I wish to thank all who opened your homes to be photographed and who then welcomed me back on subsequent visits. My heartfelt thanks to all who so willingly shared your concepts of personal space, including Christina Welty, Pamela and Royal Rowe, Bill Dalton, Janet DeNeefe and Ketut Suardana, Tony Gwilliam, Sana Hiromi and Made Sudiana Bendesa, Marita Vidal, Jacqueline Wales and Marty Reubin, Michael Pritchard, Frank Olcvary, Tony Harrison and Sheila Haisfield. Also to Made Sudiana Bendesa for sharing his knowledge of wood, woodcarving and building techniques.

Thank you, Ni. Ibu Wayan Muklin and I. Ketut Krinting, owners of Laka Leke Restaurant, for your generous assistance while photographing the restaurant. To Ibu Wayan Muklin, accomplished cook and keeper of Balinese *adat*, *budaya* and *agama*, who taught me much. Also, thank you to I. Maunde, general manager and director of so many things at Laka Leke, for making our work easier and providing me with valuable information. We are grateful to Ibu Wayan and her staff for treating us to a delicious lunch with many traditional Balinese dishes following the cooking school session. Ibu Wayan's famous chicken curry, *sayur urab*, *bergedel*, *satay litel* and *nasi goreng* are flavours extraordinaire.

To Tjokorde Gede Putra who, as always, willingly met with me to discuss Bali and Ubud's challenges in the coming years. He also opened Puri Saren in Ubud for our coverage and I am grateful for this assistance. And to Agung Rai of the Agung Rai Museum of Art, who spent hours discussing the Balinese culture… thank you Agung Rai.

Thank you, Pande Sutawan for arranging rooms at Hotel Tjampuhan for our editors visiting from Singapore, and we also appreciate the assistance of I. Ketut Karta and I. Eustace during their stay. To Ms. Lucienne Anhar at the Hotel Tugu Bali, who was of great assistance in identifying Indonesian artefacts and making our stay at Hotel Tugu a most pleasant experience.

To so many other people who gave of their time and assistance, Jay and I are grateful to all of you. Especially to I. Komang Sudarsana, our driver, translator, computer techie, photographer's assistant and resident botanist… a man of so many talents. You were not only extraordinarily helpful, your thoughtful considerations made our work comfortable and fun.

Introduction

The island of Bali is a world unto its own, a place far different from any other. Balinese cosmology explains the nature of its being as the 'centre of the world' with the sacred mountain, Gunung Agung, as the 'navel of the world'. Indian Prime Minister Jawaharlal Nehru (1889–1964) visited Bali and coined the phrase 'Bali, the morning of the world'. None of these lofty explanations seems less than real when experiencing the island first-hand. As anthropologist Geoffrey Gorer wrote in 1936:

> Bali is a small and mountainous island lying to the east
> of Java. I went there half-unwillingly, for I expected an
> uninteresting piece of bali-hoo, picturesque and faked to
> a Hollywood standard; I left wholly unwillingly, convinced
> that I had seen the nearest approach to that Utopia I am
> ever likely to see.

More recently others have written about coming to Bali, full of doubts of a place with such an enchanted name and believing they may be disappointed with the island. They leave Bali filled with wonder and somewhat doubting the rest of the world.

The beautiful gardens and moats surrounding Pura Taman Ayun, Mengwi, make this one of Bali's most beautiful temples and a favourite gathering place for families to spend an afternoon. Young boys like to fish in the moats while parents visit with friends or as these young girls have done, pose for a picture in the *bale patok* pavilion in the outer courtyard.

Bali is an incredibly beautiful island with the Indian Ocean to the south and the Bali Sea to the north. Narrow straits separate Bali from the island of Java on the west and the island of Lombok on the east. One of more than 17,500 islands and islets in the Indonesian archipelago, Bali is a small island of approximately 5560 square kilometres. It is especially small when compared to other islands of Indonesia, such as Kalimantan (Borneo) at 540,000 square kilometres or Sulawesi at 189,216 square kilometres. Java island, although smaller than Kalimantan and Sulawesi at 132,187 square kilometres, is the political centre of all Indonesia.

The name Indonesia has its roots in two Greek words: *Indos*, which means 'Indian' and *Nesos*, which means 'islands'. Early history named this group of islands 'Further India' and during the Dutch colonization, it was known as the 'East Indies'. Together, the islands of Indonesia make up the fourth most populated nation in the world. More than 88 percent of Indonesians are Muslim; however the people of Bali are mostly Hindu.

Bali's position just eight degrees below the equator assures a climate of near constant temperatures year round. Blessed with warm tropical rains and incredibly fertile, volcanic enriched soils, all of nature supports the abundance of tropical flora and fauna on the island. These natural attributes create an amazingly lush and verdant landscape that is well suited for extensive wet-rice cultivation. However, the completion of this beautiful paradise and the quality that sets it apart from any other place on earth rests with the people—the Balinese.

The Balinese are energetic and joyful people, tirelessly engaged in maintaining their cultural identity. Their rich and multi-layered culture has been developed through the centuries and remains a living culture, honoured every day through ritual observance and dedication. Through ages of invasions by warring outsiders, foreign traders, European colonialists and most recently, hordes of tourists, the Balinese have tenaciously guided their future while preserving their social order. Open to new ideas from the outside world, they distinguished the ideas workable within their belief system and then creatively turned the new concepts into acceptable forms. New ideas are

merged with the Balinese ways and take on an identity that can only be recognized as pure Balinese. Archaeologist A. J. Bernet Kempers writes in *Monumental Bali*:

> As a people, the Balinese engaged everything with which they came into contact, carefully choosing what they wanted and rejecting what they did not want after trying it out, thus creating a civilization of their own.

As revealed in early *lontar* (palm leaf) books and copper plates, the Balinese civilization evolved over a recorded history of more than two millennium. These early written treasures tell of the social history of the Balinese and discuss the rules of their social order such as regulations for the *subak* organization, their special cooperative societies that control the system of irrigation for wet-rice cultivation. This gravity-fed irrigation system, still in use today, provides water to Bali's extravagantly beautiful and productive rice terraces.

Here on this magical island is an architecture that is a tangible reflection of the true nature of the artistic, social and religious character of the Balinese. Bali is a place of communal life, where there is a sharing of religious obligations, work and social responsibility to the immediate family and the broad family of the village. The architecture that developed from this communal philosophy is one of open gathering places. Structures are not particularly for sheltering but provide environments to assemble for communal events. Balinese gathering places are therefore spaces for the convening of the family and for the village to congregate; they are places to welcome the gods and, most recently, places for tourists.

During the Galungan holiday, children's gamelan groups march through village streets playing traditional percussion rhythms using cymbals and gongs. Their very own miniature *barong* gambols along, its frolicking movements controlled by a young boy in the upper body and another in the back.

Candi Tebing in the village of Jukut Paku, Singakerta, near Ubud. This ancient rock-cut *candi* on the bank of the Wos River exemplifies the monumental style of Bali, dating between the prehistory period and the arrival of the Majapahit kingdom in the 14th century. Many *candi* of this type have been found on Bali and are believed to have been used by Buddhist monks or religious ascetics.

TWO THOUSAND YEARS OF BALINESE ARCHITECTURE

Before the arrival of Westerners on Bali, there were two recognized periods or styles of architecture, generally referred to as 'before Majapahit' and 'after Majapahit'. The earlier more monumental style is known as the Bali Aga style. It is a style of imposing, monolithic simplicity dating from Bali's pre-history period. Many ancient stone monuments scattered across Bali, such as the stepped pyramids of the mother-temple Pura Besakih on the slopes of Gunung Agung, are from the Bali Aga period. In the area of Gianyar, geographic centre of the early Pejeng-Bedulu kingdom, are numerous monumental stone-cut *candis* dating from the 10th century. *Candis* are thought to be memorials to deified royalty and are usually erected near natural springs or in deep river ravines. The *candi* at the Gunung Kawi complex in Tampaksiring is a wondrous ancient site accessed by a long stairway carved through solid rock, where one passes by a series of cell-like niches thought to have once been inhabited by monks.

People living in the villages of Tenganan, Penglipuran and Bayung Gede today proudly regard themselves as Bali Aga people (which literally translated means 'mountain people') and live lifestyles somewhat different from the general population of Bali. Their religious beliefs are more closely tied to Animism and their architectural style is devoid of the richly embellished ornamentation of the next period, the Majapahit-influenced era. The style of elaborately carved temple gates layered with mystical figures, textures and patterns usually associated with Bali's vast number of temples is one that developed after the Majapahit Hindu-Javanese kingdom migrated to Bali in the early 14th century. This highly decorative style, which is applied to architectural structures of every description and occurs in the visual arts, is easily recognized and regarded as 'the Balinese style'.

When a large population of the Royal Majapahit society—numbering in the thousands—fled to Bali to escape the autocratic penetration of Islam on Java, they brought with them their court musicians, painters, stone and wood carvers, architects, skilled workmen and priests. Their arrival gave new impetus to a society already influenced by foreign traders and Hindu mystics. A period of artistic endeavour began, one that is regarded as a golden age in Bali's history. The Balinese eagerly adapted the new ideas into all of their arts, reaching a peak of creativity as they melded and fitted the forms to suit their own methods and needs. The Balinese culture we know today is a result of the Majapahit period layered upon the Bali Aga period.

Triwangsa The concept of *triwangsa* divides society into three main castes: the Brahmans (the priestly caste); the Ksatriyas (royal families); and the Wesyas (upper middle classes). The common people of Bali are called the Sudras. While the caste system established certain rules for the society, there was never a strict or unchangeable system such as that of the 'untouchables' in India.

In addition to its contribution to Bali's architectural expression, the Majapahit migration might have also been the catalyzing influence of Hinduism upon the Balinese, who were previously practising a mixture of animism and Buddhism. Traders from India and China had already introduced the Balinese to other religious ideas and political systems, but it was the Majapahit society that brought the concept of *triwangsa*—the three privileged castes—to the island.

Balinese society is a tightly knit, collective organization that spends little to no time considering caste rules especially within their social and political organization, the village *banjar*. The *banjar* is somewhat like a volunteer social organization but one with important and far-reaching impact upon the villages, the personal lives of villagers and all of Bali. Every town is divided into small hamlets called *banjars*. At a local level, members of the hamlet administer the *banjar* and it is the *banjar* that organizes and defines much of Bali's society. *Banjars* consist of a member from each household of the hamlet who meet on a regular basis to make political decisions as well as to discuss issues regarding *adat*, *budaya* and *agama*—three key principles that have governed Balinese society.

Adat, Budaya, Agama — Principles of Balinese society

Adat (customary law), *budaya* (customs) and *agama* (religion) are three words in the language of Bali that explain much of the island's culture and the way its people have developed. Simple as these principles sound, they have governed the development of a society that is richly layered and complex (and perhaps illusive to the Western mind). Although the hold of *adat*, *budaya* and *agama* on Balinese society has been threatened by the arrival of European adventurers and Dutch colonialists in the mid-1600s, and then by the influx of tourists since the 1920s, these age-old principles still govern social behaviour and culture with remarkable consistency. Credit must be given here to the Balinese Agama-Hindu religion, which

Adat, budaya, agama — the Balinese philosophy for guidance

Adat (customary law) is concerned with the governing rules, giving structure to Balinese society. *Budaya* (customs) dictates the rules to sustain the Balinese culture. *Agama* (religion) is the Balinese Agama-Hindu religion itself, with its own defining set of rules and principles. These three words guide the Balinese each day in sustaining their magnificently rich and living culture. *Adat, budaya* and *agama* have defined the Balinese way of life and social order; it is a communal philosophy that has nourished its people.

is faithfully practised by some 95 percent of the island's inhabitants and provides a foundation for a social culture structured on religious ideals. Agama-Hindu is recognized as a religion particular to the people of Bali; it is their own and one that developed through centuries of adaptation. The religion is not just 'part of life' but 'is the life' on Bali. Philosophical and religious concepts are so intertwined in the whole of society that it is impossible to discuss the arts without including the spiritual ethics.

For more than ten centuries, the clearly defined principles of *adat, budaya* and *agama* provided the guiding force in the development of unique forms of visual and performance arts as well as a remarkably refined architecture. The people's faithful adherence to the customs, customary law and religious principles resulted in a unified culture with a distinct Balinese architecture shaped by their strong need for divine spiritual and spatial orientation.

Balinese architecture evolved from the people's social needs, becoming an indigenous architecture of spaces and structures designed specifically for convening or gathering. Their architectural art speaks a language of the people—an architecture that communicates their love for drama, their sense of humour and joy in the seemingly capricious ornamentation, and their reverence for nature while observing spiritual and spatial orientation principles required by tradition for a feeling of well-being and good health. Their building art developed with a preponderance of religious requirements but was also influenced by other factors such as the hot, humid equatorial climate, the building materials available as well as techniques that could be accomplished by hand.

There is a new style of architecture in Bali today, a new building art with adapted components of traditional Balinese forms that fit the needs and design aesthetics of a modern world. This book will show you not only the 'gathering places' of traditional Bali but also the 'gathering places' of modern Bali. All represent Balinese architecture at its finest, solving the requirements of shelter while sensitively answering the need for creative and dynamic space. Balinese architecture is defined and enriched by the multi-layered expressions of *adat, budaya* and *agama* that are all clearly manifested in the architecture of gathering and convening—Gathering Places.

The time has come to go to temple for a ceremony. The community has finished decorating every available edifice with colourful fabrics, all statues are dressed in *poleng* cloth sarongs, umbrellas are in place and now, village women and children begin to arrive dressed in their very best *adat* clothing. The woman on the left has placed her offering in a *sok* basket; the other woman carries a tall offering made from fresh fruits and flowers.

TAMAT.   13-9-1954

Spiritual gathering places

Where one's mind is attached—the inner self
Goes thereto with action, being attached to it alone
Obtaining the end of his action,
Whatever he does in this world,
He comes again from that world [the realm of the dead]
To this world of action.

— From the *Upanishads* regarding Karma

AGAMA HINDU BALI

The entire island of Bali is a spiritual gathering place. On any day, somewhere on Bali, there are gatherings where an entire village joyfully comes together to participate in a communal event, gathering in preparation for a temple ceremony or gathering to pay homage to the gods. The gathering places for these ceremonies are Bali's precious architectural heritage—its temples or *pura*. Balinese temples use the celestial heavens as a roof to cover sacred space, the open-air courtyards. The grand entry gates that lead into these ceremonial courtyards, delineated by low walls and filled with shrines and *bale* (pavilions), are the incomparable architectural designs so easily recognized as uniquely Balinese.

LEFT The *kulkul* tower of Pura Taman Ayun at Mengwi is completely decorated for an upcoming Galungan celebration. Even the two large hollow wood *kulkul* inside it are wrapped in *poleng* cloth and saffron coloured cloth. The carved stone decorations are a traditional architectural style from the Majapahit era.

ABOVE Poised and elegant, this lady goes to temple with her hair styled as carefully as the offering she has made. Sitting among the offering of fruit is a small jar of water; both the fruit and water will be blessed by the priest. Once blessed, the fruit will be taken back to the family compound to be eaten and the holy water will be used in the family temple or sprinkled on offerings placed around the compound.

A unity of religious ideals created the architectural art form of the temples, an architecture that clearly represents the true nature of the people and their social character. Balinese architecture is a tangible reflection of the Balinese spiritual consciousness.

Spirituality and the metaphysical world, that 'other world' of mystics, are accepted by the Balinese as absolute and ever-present. *Sekala* and *niskala*—of this world and the opposite unseen world—are part of life here. Illusions are real but real only as opposed to the unreality of all things. The neither-nor, where good is neither good nor bad, creates a search for balance and for Oneness. It is the search for balance and harmony that creates the constant busyness seen in Bali: the daily making of offerings, the performance of rituals and the desire to make every effort to please the gods. There is an attitude of giving more than taking, of honouring nature and the oneness of the Universe. From the busy streets of beachside tourist resorts, such as Kuta, Seminyak or Sanur, to the most remote mountain villages, processions and ceremonies are a daily occurrence, an act of giving back to the Universe.

This island society is devoted to the spiritual principles of Agama-Hindu, the Balinese religion. Agama-Hindu principles formed a historic structure for the society and have remained the binding source of inspiration for the people. Yet it is not a dogmatic religion; it continues to change and blend as new ideas seem appropriate. Agama-Hindu is a combination of three belief systems: Animism, Buddhism and Hinduism. It is a Balinese invention, an adaptation, a creation of their own and one so characteristic of the people. It is a classic representation of their discriminating way of sorting, adapting and combining foreign ideas to suit their needs.

The magnificent *paduraksa* (monumental) gate in the village of Satria, near Klungkung, makes an elegantly imposing backdrop for the dance performance that is to take place in the outer courtyard.

Stylish embellishments date this monumental gate in a temple in the village of Iseh to before the Majapahit period, which began from the 14th century. The many stone steps are an indication of the monolithic period of Bali's history.

Subak organizations These special cooperative societies administer affairs relating to agriculture, most importantly the allocation of water for the irrigation of rice fields. This highly sophisticated system delivers water through a labyrinth of small canals and sluiceways, is completely gravity-fed and is the same irrigation system today as the system in place, according to recorded history, from 300 BC.

Agama-Hindu is historically called 'Agama Tirta', which means 'religion of water'. An old *lontar* tells of a pilgrimage made by an Indian sage, Rsi Markandeya, in the eighth century. During his journey he was drawn to a centre of powerful energy at the confluence of two rivers, the Tjampuhan River and the Wos River in the village of Campuhan. He built a temple there and then many other temples along the Wos River, including a temple to Wishnu—the god of water—thereby naming the religion Agama Tirta. Rsi Markandeya is credited by historians as the first to bring not only the principles of Hinduism to Bali but also the philosophy of *tri hita karana*, or the 'three causes of goodness', as well as the important concept of the *subak* organization that oversees the irrigation of rice fields, a process still used in modern Bali today. Although the principles of Hinduism were brought to Bali by Rsi Markandeya, sages and priests have expanded these ideas through the centuries and continue to do so today.

Agama Tirta is an appropriate name for this religion since holy water is literally sprinkled at every opportunity on objects and offerings and always on worshippers as they pray. There are vast numbers of ancient stone watering places where natural spring waters gush from rock crevices or wells. These sites are considered sacred since flowing water is living water and hence believed to be the magic of life. The springs are both gathering places for cleansing rituals and collecting sites for the holy water used in temples and other ceremonies. A stone inscription in the old Balinese language dates the sacred bathing pools of Tirta Empul near Tampaksiring at AD 960.

Like holy water, Bali is sprinkled with thousands of *pura* or temples. Some say the *pura* were broadcast like seeds by the gods since they are literally scattered everywhere. In every town or village there are at least three separate temples: the *pura desa* (town temple), the *pura puseh* (temple of origin) and the *pura dalem* (temple of the dead or ancestors).

There are temples within the walls of every family compound, temples in the rice fields, temples for the *subak* organization, temples for the hills, temples for the rivers; it is almost impossible to list them all. The most important temple on Bali, however, is Pura Besakih high up on the slopes of Gunung Agung. It was named the State Temple in the 13th century and remains the mother temple of the island. It is not one temple but a large complex of temples. Annual pilgrimages to Pura Besakih are made by most Balinese, as well as village groups who arrive throughout the year to pray and collect holy water for rituals in their local village *pura*. The sight of a large ceremony at Pura Besakih is a major extravaganza of beauty and remarkable pageantry.

The priest pronounced long mantras and steadied their prayers with the single silvery ringing of his hand bell. Each by each they picked up a blossom and, passing it through a waft of incense, raised it to their foreheads holding it in their fingertips and sending their prayers adorned in scent on the carriage of flowers and mantra and scented smoke—for that is how the gods of Bali are addressed. First a red blossom to Bhatara Guru; then a white one to Bhatara Iswara, then a yellow one to the gods of Gunung Agung.

From The Painted Alphabet *by Diana Darling*

Sacred banyan trees In front of every village temple there is usually a plot of land which serves as a village gathering place. On it is a *wantilan,* an open-air social hall with a soaring roof of thatch, and an ancient *beringin,* or banyan, tree that is a symbol of the family and therefore considered sacred.

Mature banyan trees have many auxiliary trunks resulting from hair-like roots that reach the ground from large spreading branches. Nourishment and support are given to the old tree from the family of trunks—just like the Balinese family structure. Some very old banyan trees no longer have a central trunk but continue to live through its many rooted branches. *Beringin* trees are often dressed with a sarong of *poleng* cloth around the trunk and are bedecked with small temporary bamboo shrines for the placement of offerings. *Poleng* is the white- and black-checked woven fabric seen wrapped around statues and is also used as a stylish waist cloth for men. Symbolically the white checks of the *poleng* represent good; the black indicates opposing forces; and the grey where the fibres blend indicates balance or the desired harmony.

Temple ceremonies and religious rituals are completely embedded with a magnificent beauty. Reverence and devotion are undisguised; the basic dedication of offerings to the gods is a brief part of the overall celebration. Much more evident and apparently most meaningful is the coming together of the community to prepare and present the rituals with days and weeks filled with busy activity—all hands are needed and engaged. Temple ceremonies are whole-hearted celebrations, filled with joy and an effervescence of spirit. They are true gathering places for the village to welcome the gods and for the people to be with each other in a communal event.

Although temple designs vary from the north of Bali to the south and from village to village, there is still much similarity in their layout. All have courtyards that are open to the sky and to all of nature, a fine characterization of the Balinese Agama-Hindu religion: the gaiety and light-hearted atmosphere of a temple ceremony requires an unenclosed architecture that relates to nature.

An old banyan tree has lost its central trunk but the family branches continue the life of the tree. Shrines dressed in *poleng* cloth often have an umbrella—an invitation to the gods to come and rest.

DIVINE OUTDOOR SPACE — THE PURA

The walls surrounding Bali's open-air cathedrals create sacred inner spaces— courtyards in the splendid out-of-doors, a feature that stands in distinction from the enclosed interior space of Western cathedrals. Each Balinese temple has two courtyards with a variety of *bale*, or pavilions, shrines and small buildings to accommodate different activities. Each courtyard, in turn, has a specific function.

The first courtyard of a temple is accessed through a split-gate called the *candi bentar*. *Candi bentar* are said to suggest hands held in prayer. Once one has climbed the stairs and entered through the gate, the profane world is left behind and *adat* (customary law) clothing is required to enter the temple. Women must wear the traditional sarong, a *kebaya* (blouse of a certain style) and a scarf tied about the waist. Although not required, the custom is for women to wear their hair twisted in a stylish way with fresh flowers tucked behind the ear or in a comb at the back of the head, as well as lovely make-up and their best jewellery. Men wear a sarong tied in the front so that the fabric falls in a dashing manner, a *saput* (short waist cloth of contrasting pattern and colour) around the waist, a shirt and a head-dress. Processions are a magnificent sight, with children dressed as their parents, all walking along in a gorgeous array of colours and patterns, the sound of gongs, cymbals and drums elevating the excitement. Going to the temple is not a time to humble oneself but a time to welcome the gods with beautiful sights and sounds.

Just inside the first courtyard stands a tall *kulkul* tower with hollow tubes made of wood or bamboo. The *kulkul* is a drum used for sending messages to the villagers. Also in this courtyard are open *bale* for the making of offerings or food for feasts; the *bale gong* to house the gamelan orchestra; and *bale* for resting.

Aling-aling *Aling-aling* are stone or brick walls placed immediately inside the *paduraksa* gate. They are usually highly ornamented with carvings, often including the awesomely scary face of Boma (man of the forest) with bulging eyes, a gaping mouth and protruding fangs. Should the Boma fail to discourage malevolent spirits, the *aling-aling* stands ready to protect the sacred courtyard even further from such spirits, which are believed to be able to only travel a straight path, being unable to turn corners.

At the back of the first courtyard is a taller, more monumental gate called the *paduraksa* or *kori agung*, which leads into the most sacred area of the temple. The gate has an impressive central flight of stairs leading up to a main door reserved for use by the gods or by a procession carrying special offerings

LEFT This *kulkul* tower at Pura Desa Lukluk is completely covered with stone carvings.

ABOVE Looking over the wall towards the *paduraksa* gate is the innermost sacred courtyard of a small and very old temple. *Ijuk* (fibre from the sugar-palm tree) or *alang-alang* (grass) thatching have succumbed to the more economical corrugated steel roofs in this temple.

and shrines in which the gods might be resting. The *paduraksa* may also be used by the *barong*; this larger than life-sized monstrous looking puppet with a shaggy mane and bulging eyes represents a mythical animal held sacred for its ability to mediate between good and evil (a variation of the Chinese dragon or Vietnamese Kylin). Two men are required to propel the loveable creature—one in the head and upper body and the other in the hindquarters. Worshippers must enter the temple's most sacred area through two smaller doors located at a lower level on either side of the main door. Upon passing

through the doors of the gate, they are confronted by the *aling-aling*, a wall built to prevent malevolent energies from entering the temple, making it is necessary to turn left or right around the wall to proceed further.

A variety of small buildings, *bale* and shrines can be found in this most sacred area, although the placement of these structures and their numbers differ for each village to suit local needs. One such building is the *gedong pasimpangan*, used for honouring deities and for storing temple heirlooms. Another *bale* located in this area is for priests to make offerings or prayers. A shrine called the *padmasana* is always placed in the northeastern corner of the temple, the most sacred location, and is usually reserved for the Sun god, Surya, or for the Hindu holy trinity, the *Trisakti* comprising Brahma, Siwa and Wishnu. *Padmasana* are shrines without symbolic or statuary representation of the gods and are empty to provide places for the gods to visit and rest. Often the most beautiful shrines in the compound are the *meru*. These are pagoda-shaped structures with uneven numbers of roofs—either three, five, seven, nine or eleven—each ever diminishing in size from bottom to top. The roofs are made of *ijuk*, a long-lasting black fibre made from the sugar-palm tree. *Meru* symbolize the cosmic mountain Mahameru, which the Balinese believe to be the axis of the universe. Like the *padmasana* shrines, *meru* are also empty shrines—a towering open shaft waiting for the invited gods to enter.

BALINESE ARCHITECTURE: A SPIRITUAL AND SPATIAL ORIENTATION

All of life on Bali is based on the ideals of cosmological orientation, a divine cosmic order and a metaphysical understanding of how correct placement results in harmony and balance. Every part of the natural world has an order divided into three parts: *Utama* is high or above where all things sacred and pure abide; *madya* is the middle area, the mundane world where humans exist; and then there is *nista*, a low, unclean netherworld.

There are always divisions of three in the various philosophies of Bali where the middle, as in the human world, plays a role of balancing the antagonists and the opposition. *Adat, budaya and agama* provide a foundation of rules and laws for the Balinese society while *tri hita karana* (the 'three causes of goodness') is concerned with achieving equilibrium in life. The essence of this philosophy provides instruction on how to find a balance of life and harmony of relationships: people with God, people with nature and people with others. In a speech of love and brotherhood—one that expressed a message from the heart of the Balinese people to the people of the world—given in the aftermath of the terrorist bomb attack in Kuta, Asana Viebeke said:

"We Balinese have an essential concept of balance. It's the Tri Hita Karana; a concept of harmonious balance. The balance between god and humanity; humanity with itself and humanity with the environment. This places us all in a universe of common understanding."

— Asana Viebeke is spokesperson for *Parum Samigita*, the 'think tank' for the village councils, the Banjars of the Kuta, Legian and Seminyak areas of Bali. 23 October 2005

Always a triad, a division of three—even the philosophies number 'three' for accompanying and reinforcing the concepts of *adat, budaya* and *agama*—there is also *tri hita karana* and then there is *tri angga*. Maintaining the three-fold concept, *tri angga* explains a hierarchy of space by dividing the physical world into three zones known collectively as the *tri loka*, which includes *swah loka* (atmosphere), *bhuwah loka* (lithosphere) and *bhur loka* (hydrosphere). The three zones relate to high, middle and low respectively, as on Earth where they correspond to mountains (high), land (middle) and sea (low). The people of Bali are among the few island people of the world who turn towards the mountains rather than to the sea. They believe that gods and goddesses inhabit the mountains while other spirits, good or bad, dwell in the ocean depths. People living between the sea and mountains must therefore find a balance between these two opposing forces. Even the human form is part of this cosmological framework: head (high), torso (middle), feet (low). The Balinese say they have restless sleep and feel disoriented if they do not sleep with their heads facing North or to the East. They believe it is disrespectful to point the feet towards the mountains in the North where the gods dwell, as the feet are considered an unclean part of the body. Furthermore, patting or touching a child on the head, which Western people often affectionately do, is not a welcomed gesture on Bali.

The natural world of the Balinese is intertwined with metaphysical explanations that form the underlying principles in their architecture. Mountain-sea (North-South) and sunrise-sunset (East-West) are the most influential axes with the directions towards the great mountain Gunung Agung being the more

Gunung Agung, the spiritual centre of Bali.

Spiritual compass points: Orientation towards the mountain or sea Most of the land mass of Bali lies to the south of Gunung Agung. Therefore, the Balinese orientation 'towards the North', in essence really towards the mountain, is the most sacred point. However, for the people living north of Gunung Agung, they would reverse these orientations so that 'towards the South' is most sacred to them.

sacred of these two axes. As a result, cardinal compass points and the principles of *tri angga* are utilized in temple layouts and in the layouts of village streets and compounds. The spatial orientation of villages is on a North-South axis with the more sacred temple, the *pura puseh* (temple of origin), located towards the mountain while the *pura dalem* (temple of the dead) and the cemetery are located away from the mountain. The centre of the village, the 'body' of the village, is where the markets and the *puri*, or palace, are located.

Many symbolic devices in temple architecture further emphasize the principles of *tri angga*, establishing the role of the universe and the worshippers within a macrocosm-microcosm of space. Each courtyard in temples is higher in elevation than the previous. Celebrants move upward through gates, ascending flights of stairs to leave the mundane world behind to enter more sacred space. The first courtyard is for reverent community activities, unlike the second courtyard (the more sacred inner space) which can only be reached by moving upward, an act that requires concerted physical action to move closer to the divine. In this way, the basic floor

Living structures Divine cosmic order provides the guidelines for placement, describing how each part relates to all other parts and where the microcosm and macrocosm become an integrated whole when qualified by the animistic traditions of early Bali. An *undagi* (architect who is also a priest) is called to site a new building for harmonious placement and to choose an auspicious day for each stage of construction. He also takes body measurements of the head of the household, which he uses to plan and design the building. Using animistic principles that centre on the belief that animate and inanimate objects have an innate soul, structural posts (from coconut, bamboo or posts of other species of wood) are erected as they grew. These posts are floated in a stream, the heavier end will sink lower into the water, thus the root end can be determined so the posts may be installed in a position of natural growth. The *undagi* performs ceremonies throughout the construction as well as completion ceremonies when the building is finished. The final ceremony is to breathe life into the materials once again, making the structure a living organic whole. Only then is the building ready to be occupied. One final placement is required before a building is deemed to be fully completed—the roof must have a decorative crown, like a hat protecting the head. This decorative element is usually made of terracotta, shaped like a crown and placed at the top of a hip-roof or somewhere along the ridge on gabled roofs. In beachside communities, coconuts are frequently halved and placed on the entire ridge of the roof. These final touches have a practical purpose in that they help to drain rainwater away, preventing leaks at the point where roofing materials form a peak.

Weathered blue paint on these shrines in a family temple add a bit of whimsy in this sacred area. Black *ijuk* thatch is from the sugar-palm tree. The decorative crown, a *Karang Murdha*, can be seen on the shrine towards the back.

plan of temples develop a connection between the cosmology of the temple and the universe; between the relationship of worshipers and that greater universe; and establishes a tie within the people's own universe (the community), which is their own personal miniature world.

Even the design and layout of family compounds follow similar orientations. As described by the spiritual compass points called *nawa sanga* or *sanga mandala,* sleeping rooms are located in the middle of the compound, family temples are placed towards the mountain, and kitchens and animal pens are located in a lower area and directionally to the west .

The philosophy of *tri angga* and its effect on spatial orientation is further expanded when using the spiritual compass points to determine cosmological orientation. The compass consists of eight cardinal directions and one central or focal point, making a total of nine compass points. Part of the decision on where a building is placed is determined by the eventual use of the building, for instance a pig pen must be in the southwest. Where offerings or foods prepared for ritual are concerned, the ingredients must have colours corresponding to those of the deity being honoured as specified by the *sanga* mandala (See the Architectural Notebook section for further information on the subject of *tri angga* and *sanga* mandala or *nawa sanga*.)

THE ART OF TEMPLE CEREMONIES

A leaf, a flower, a fruit or even water
Offered to me in devotion, I will accept as
The loving gift of a dedicated heart.
Whatever you do, Make it an offering to me—
The food you eat or Worship you perform,
The help you give, even your suffering.
Thus will you be free from Karma's bondage,
From the results of action, good and bad.

— Upanishads: The Bhagavad Gita

The ceremonies and rituals required in daily life have provided a platform for and stimulated the expression of the artistic nature of the Balinese. Constant rounds of temple festivities require performances in music, drama and dance to entertain the gods. Offerings of fresh flowers and fruits are made for the gods at every ceremony and there are special occasions that require offerings to be made of brightly coloured designs from rice paste or from the stomachs of pigs, the latter having a delicate white lace-like appearance. And then there are the exquisitely prepared *canang,* or woven basket offerings, which are made daily and filled with flowers and sweet smelling grasses to be placed here and there and everywhere, or the woven *lamak* or arching *penjors.* While such activities are a temporary and transient form of art, they are incredibly beautiful and artistically conceived and constructed. The festivities, the ceremonies with their rituals of performance, the decorations of temples and offerings... all these demand artistic endeavour of everyone in a never-ending calendar of events.

During Galungan holy days, which occur twice a year in the Balinese calendar of 210 days, streets are lined with *penjors.* The men of each compound decorate these tall, arching bamboo poles with fresh sheaves of rice, flowers, coconuts and images of the rice goddess, Dewi Sri. *Penjors* represent the tall mountains and are decorated to give thanks for all of Earth's bounty. The Balinese calendar is completely filled with special days of temple ceremonies, all requiring skillful, artistic work to complete and fulfill the many obligations. Dancers and musicians meet and rehearse many times each week in preparation to entertain the gods at temple festivities. Most temples have an abundant array of ancient *batu paras* (sandstone) carvings and statues, all requiring constant restoration or replacement due to the ravages of a tropical climate on the soft stone. Skilled artisans are called upon to complete the renovations, generating a practical need for carvers and builders. There is a symbiosis between the artists and the temple activities: artists are required to provide for the various needs or ceremonies for the temple and the artistic expression of the people has a venue.

Reincarnation—cycles of birth and rebirth—is not a subject of debate or discussion but an actuality in the Balinese belief. Death is not a feared, final state but the recurring of life until a glorious state of *moksa* (release from the cycle of rebirth; a positive state of completion free from karma) is attained. After this perfection, one reaches nirvana and union with the Supreme. Theories that are abstract to Western people are accepted by the Balinese as absolute and require no deliberation. Cosmological beliefs and the spatial orientation philosophies along with ancestor worship strengthen the need for many ceremonies and rituals, and therein lie the purpose of the daily practice of beliefs that keep the Balinese culture true to itself.

Pura Taman Ayun, Mengwi

Pura Taman Ayun in Mengwi is considered to be one of Bali's most beautiful temples. It was built in 1634 by the Raja of Mengwi, I. Gusti Agung Ngurah Made Agung, as a place of worship for his royal ancestors and is representative of the highly decorative and formal Majapahit style of the time, which had reached a high point in this architectural period. Surrounded by two separate moats and graced with trees that bear fruit and sweet smelling flowers, Pura Taman Ayun is a place of quiet serenity although its history has been less than calm.

Mengwi was one of nine kingdoms in early Bali. For centuries, the kingdoms were at war, first with each other and then later, with the Dutch. The temple buildings deteriorated during this long period of unrest until 1911, when part of the royal family of Mengwi returned to their family property and set about restoring the temple. Unfortunately, a violent earthquake in 1917 damaged many of the structures. Since then, repairs and renovations have been ongoing to restore them to their original condition and design. The royal family of Puri Gede Mengwi continues to maintain the temple with assistance from the local district of Mengwi.

Both the first and second courtyards at Pura Taman Ayun are surrounded by a moat. A bridge constructed of concrete and stone leads to the *candi bentar*. The large roof to the right belongs to the *wantilan agung*, the king's social hall used for public gatherings.

LEFT The *wantilan agung* at Pura Taman Ayun is a treasure. Preserved in its original state, wood posts and beams joined by bamboo pegs support the double-tiered *alang-alang* roof. The floor is stepped down for use as tiered seating for watching dance and drama performances, shadow puppet plays or ritual cockfights. This structure is the essence of a gathering place for it is a social hall for all of Mengwi. On this day, men of the local *banjar* are using the *wantilan* to make *penjors* for the Galungan celebration.

TOP A view upward from inside the *kulkul* tower. Large wooden cylinders are struck to send messages to the villagers of Mengwi.

BOTTOM View of the *candi bentar* leading into the first courtyard of Pura Taman Ayun, which has a park-like setting.

RIGHT A shrine in the first courtyard at Pura Taman Ayun is being decorated by a *pemangku*, or village priest, for a ceremony. He is adjusting a *lamak*, a long mat of young palm fronds which are dyed and then intricately woven into designs related to the rice goddess Dewi Sri. *Lamak* are woven on special occasions to decorate the entry to temples and family compounds.

OPPOSITE This grand *paduraksa* entry to the second courtyard is elegantly proportioned and embellished in the highly decorative Majapahit style. It was built in 1634, at the height of the Majapahit period in Bali. The men in front of the gate prepare to erect a *penjor* they have made for the Galungan ceremony.

OPPOSITE View of the magnificent Majapahit *paduraksa* at Pura Taman Ayun. The moat continues around the perimeter of this sacred inner courtyard.

LEFT *Meru* in the most sacred courtyard of Pura Taman Ayun. The eleven-tiered *meru* in the foreground represents Pura Besakih, the mother temple.

ABOVE *Meru* are shafts to the heavens; they open down the middle so the gods may enter and rest during temple ceremonies.

Pura Penataran Sasih, Pejeng

The village of Pejeng and the region surrounding it are where some of Bali's oldest historical sites have been found. Pura Penataran Sasih was a central temple in the old kingdom of Pejeng, a historic site with a sacred inner courtyard still being used by the villagers of Pejeng. Within its sacred confines lies the earliest known pre-Hindu kettledrum, often referred to as the 'Pejeng Moon'. Balinese stories tell of the drum, which is thought to be a wheel of the moon. Spanning some 186 centimetres in diameter and probably dating from about 300 BC, it is also considered to be the largest single-cast bronze piece in the world. Drums of this type were known to be cast in Vietnam during the Dong Son Bronze Age (fourth century BC to first century AD). The Pejeng Moon drum is considered to have been cast on Bali since casting moulds have been found on the island. This historic bronze drum is kept in an open *bale* alongside other shrines and *bale* with ancient artefacts.

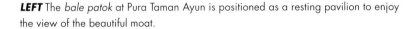

LEFT The *bale patok* at Pura Taman Ayun is positioned as a resting pavilion to enjoy the view of the beautiful moat.

TOP View of Pura Penataran Sasih's inner courtyard where the Pejeng Moon kettledrum is stored. Villagers prefer the drum not be photographed. The kettledrum is kept in an open *bale* just beyond the first *bale* on the right. All the structures in this compound have an amazingly ancient feel and are beautiful in their simplicity and tradition. Ceremonies marking the full moon are an exquisite sight to see here.

BOTTOM Ancient artefacts rather haphazardly conserved are placed at the back of Pura Penataran Sasih. The steps and platform, although restored, may be a remnant of the megalithic stepped pyramids of early Bali.

TEMPLE GATES

Highly carved *kori agung* at Pura Lukluk in the Badung region has details of the Majaphahit period but does not have the usual red brick and *paras* stone combinations seen in southern Bali.

As in Balinese paintings, not an inch of this wall is left undecorated. The view is through the *candi bentar* towards the *kori agung* at Pura Lukluk.

A plant has attached itself to the top of this old pre-Majapahit gate, located in Pura Puseh, Krobokan (near the beach area of Kuta). However, the gold-leaf door is a modern element.

An early Majapahit *kori agung* in the village of Jukut Paku, Singakerta. The *bale* in the foreground is new.

LEFT Majapahit-style *candi bentar* entrance to the outer courtyard of Pura Penataran Sasih.

This magnificent *kori agung* may have been built at the end of the Bali Aga period when the highly decorative carvings of the Majapahit style were becoming popular in the 14th and 15th centuries.

Kori agung of a family temple in the village of Negari. Fanciful *paras* stone carvings with red brick are characteristic of the Majapahit style. However, this gate is a newer adaptation.

Village gathering places

That which is the subtle essence,
In it all that exist has its self.
It is the true. It is the self.
And you, my son: tat twam asi. *

Bali's equatorial pre-dawn skies are bright long before sunrise
and just as this first morning light filters through the canopy
of large tropical trees, village life begins to stir in the family
compounds. Bali's true essence is contained within these walls
a place where grandparents, mothers and fathers, aunts and
uncles, and children of all ages live on a land handed down
through centuries of patriarchal lineage. Early morning sounds
of birds chirping and roosters crowing accompany the swish
swish-swish of stiff coconut brooms as gardens are swept. The
delicious aroma of spices sizzling in fresh coconut oil fills the
air as food preparation begins over cooking fires fueled with
coconut husks or stalks of bamboo. *Banten*, offerings of fresh
palm-leaf baskets with layers of symbolic ingredients including
bits of rice, sweet smelling flowers, grasses and leaves, are
made and placed here and there as a gift to the deities before
the family begins eating. Steamed white rice and dark rich Bali
kopi (coffee) wait in the kitchen; each person takes a portion
and sits alone to eat. Now the day can begin. The land and
the Balinese communal way of life are bound to traditions that
continue each day in this walled community.

Banten are architecturally beautiful in their designs of rice cakes, fresh fruit and
flowers. Tall fruit banten, such as the one here, are composed by piercing fruit with
bamboo skewers that are then stuck into a length of banana trunk. Every ingredient
and colour represents a different intention.

* *From Chandogya Upanishad, a dialogue between guru and student explaining the identity of Atman and Brahman.*
The student is asked to open the fruit of an almond from a nearby tree. He is asked what he sees. The student replies he
sees a nut. The teacher then asks that he open the nut and tell him what he sees. He replies he does not see anything. The
teacher replies that the subtle essence he does not see is the very essence on which the almond tree exists.... "and herein
lies the essence of the almond tree, the all, the oneness... and you, my son: this is you (tat twam asi)"

Compound walls and entry gates line the village street of Nyuh Kuning. The drainage ditch that runs along each side of the road diverts tremendous amounts of rainwater during the monsoon season.

Each walled residential compound defines the area of patriarchal lands. In practical terms, the wall also provides needed privacy and security in a densely populated society; it also helps deter neighbouring dogs from roaming around the compound. In the more rural villages, these walls are frequently made of *popolan* (adobe blocks) or plaited bamboo. The walls of more affluent villagers are highly decorative with combinations of *paras* stone (sandstone) carvings and bricks laid in patterns. In recent history, the style of a gate indicated the caste of a family but as with many caste rules in Bali,

this design restraint has now undergone change and *sudra* (common people) families may have a gate as elaborate as funds may allow.

Every gate is elevated above the street and is usually an open entryway. However, privacy is maintained by an *aling-aling*, a wall placed just inside the gate. *Aling-aling* are usually made of brick, concrete or mud and made decorative in several ways: through designs developed by using different sizes of brick; by changing the direction of brick courses; or by inserting stone carvings or insets of contrasting materials. These

Paras stone and thatch materials were used in building this handsome entry gate at Alam Indah, the homestay of Ibu Wayan and Ketut Krinting. The man at the gate, one of the staff at the homestay, is handsome as well.

An entry gate constructed of chunky sun-dried mud bricks is organically beautiful in its honesty of materials.

walls offer several advantages: they are believed to block the path of malevolent spirits from entering the compound; they add an attractive garden feature to the courtyard; they provide an interruption on arrival, a brief moment to pause before entering the compound. This single moment to stop mentally and physically allows one to leave the outside world behind and focus on the world within the compound walls.

The gathering places of village life begin in the compounds and extend out to the streets. On many mornings the *kulkul* is sounded: its hollow, low drumbeats become increasingly louder to send messages throughout the *banjar*, informing the villagers of some news or inviting them to gather at the *wantilan*, an open-air social hall, for a meeting. Quiet village lanes become busy thoroughfares as villagers emerge from the entry gates of their private compounds to begin their day.

It is on these narrow roads and lanes of provincial Balinese villages where daily life unfolds that the symbiotic nature of life on Bali is revealed. A life of social responsibility to the family and extended family of the village is not unlike the lives of their ancestors centuries before. In the morning, streets are crowded with women on their way to the market, balancing large baskets filled with produce to be sold at food stalls. Children march off to school wearing uniforms that in some villages are bright ikat-patterned vests. Farmers head to their fields past ducks waddling in single file, anxiously following the herder; farmers, ducks and herders are all on their way to the *sawah* (rice fields) for the day's work. Then there are the young people on motorbikes making their way to jobs in the tourist businesses or others with their vehicles piled high with

products to be sold at markets in the larger towns. Grandfathers tuck machetes into their sarongs and shoulder bamboo poles with baskets that they will soon fill with grass they cut along the roadside or dykes of the *sawah* to bring home to the family cow. Left behind in the compounds are grandmothers caring for the babies while dogs guard entry gates and roosters wait in their roadside baskets for the afternoon when all return and social life of the village can begin again.

ABOVE A basket maker heads to market to sell his inventory of dome-shaped homes for fighting cocks. The Balinese use split bamboo or rattan to make utilitarian baskets, stressing practicality over beauty. Nevertheless, they manage to weave an exquisite sense of texture and proportion into this applied art, resulting in a functional object of art with intrinsic value.

RIGHT A *warung*, or small food stall, set into a family's compound wall in the village of Nyuh Kuning. This stall offers snacks, drinks and plenty of conversation. It is an informal gathering place to meet and *omong-omong* (talk together); the simple architecture of the *warung* sets an atmosphere for unpretentious gatherings.

RIGHT Market day is a time of high excitement. Roads are jammed with buyers and sellers from the countryside converging into the towns. Public transport is by way of individually owned vans called *bemos*.

OPPOSITE The village *pasar* (market) finds vendors selling ingredients for offerings, such as flower petals and sweet grasses, as well as the items required to make a betel quid (betel leaf, areca nuts and lime) that are placed in most offerings. This seller weaves palm-leaf baskets for her customers who do not have sufficient time at home to make their own.

Socializing is an important part of the Balinese way of life. Therefore the communal life of the family spills out into village streets and public places: the *warungs* (food stalls), the *tokos* (shops), the *pasar* (market) and most importantly, the three village *puras* (temples) where there are continuous preparations for ceremonies—all are gathering places to socialize and chat. Throughout the day at the market, there is constant banter and camaraderie. Every rice field has a *pondok*, a small bamboo and thatch-roofed shelter, that is a place to rest and talk during the workday. Late afternoons find women gathered at their entry gates to pass news heard at the market; men gather at the *wantilan* in the village centre to share gossip; young folks gather at the volleyball courts, football fields or *bale* to play badminton. Later the *wantilan* will be filled with people practising gamelan music or learning a dance or attending a *banjar* meeting to discuss village matters.

The gathering places for village life begin in the compound then move out to the heart of the village to the village square where important public buildings are located. The planning of the village around the square follows the spiritual concept of *tri angga* with the *pura desa* (village temple) positioned on the most sacred ground, the quadrant closest to Gunung Agung. The *puri*, or palace, is located at the crossroads of the square along with the *wantilan* and the *pasar*. The centre of this crossroad is a point of significant and powerful energy. Professor Eko Budihardjo, Dean of Architecture at Diponegoro University in Java, writes in *Architectural Conservation in Bali*:

> *The village is a unified organism, in which every individual is a corpuscle and every institution is an organ. The heart of the village is the central square, invariably located at the centre of the village. The cardinal directions mean a great deal to the Balinese, and the crossroads focusing on the central square are a magic spot of great importance. All the open spaces: the square, the avenues, the streets, are in fact an extended living area where people meet each other, where all the children play, and also a place where the ceremonial feast takes place.*

Bali is a place of communal life, a sharing of religious obligations and social responsibilities to the immediate family and to the broad family of the village. The architecture that developed from this communal philosophy is one of open gathering places. Structures are not for enclosed sheltering but provide environments to assemble for communal events. An architecture of and for gathering—the compounds are for the convening of the family; the *wantilan* serve as a community hall for the meetings of the village; the temples are places for the gods to visit; and the *pura puseh* (temple of origin) and family temples in the compounds are for the visits of ancestors and deities.

ABOVE Bamboo *pondok*, built on the principles of the traditional *bale*, are scattered throughout the *sawah* for resting and communing with nature or with friends. Young rice has been recently planted; it is a beautiful time in the cycle of cultivation as the still pools reflect the landscape and sky.

OPPOSITE Women resting in a *bale* near the rice field where they have been working. Someone will hoist that heavy white bag of rice onto a woman's head and she will walk away with the grace of a runway model. Corrugated metal roofing has replaced the more expensive *alang-alang* thatch.

ABOVE Most Balinese homes are now made of concrete block with tiled roofs and ceramic tile floors. There is little to no furniture. The floors of pavilions are built 35 to 45 centimetres off the ground providing the perfect seating height. This couple lives in Pejeng—he keeps bees, raises small crops, tends his rice field and conducts tours of the nearby Pura Penataran Sasih temple; she has a bucket of tapioca for making crackers to sell at the market. Donald Duck sitting in the shrine for offerings is not irreverent but reveals the jocular Balinese way of not taking life so seriously.

LEFT Attractive and gentle Balinese faces—Made, Luhde and Dekdion.

LEFT Rice moulded into various shapes for particular offerings are carefully arranged in a basket. The message on this *ibu*'s (mother; a polite form of address) T-shirt is a vote of confidence for Indonesia's first woman president, Megawati Sukarnoputri.

BOTTOM Offerings of flowers and crispy thin bright orange cakes made of rice dough. Different ceremonies require different offerings in terms of their shape, colour and ingredients. Offerings are made of specific ingredients associated with a particular intention; even the scrambled eggs on the plate will be used as an ingredient. The complexity of all this would take a lifetime to learn.

FOLLOWING PAGES Workers select young rice seedlings to plant. Rice cultivation on Bali is a remarkable process of social organization. The *subak* authority determines which fields receive water from the irrigation system as required for the particular cycle of planting, growth or harvesting. Irrigation water flows from the north of the island to the south and is completely gravity-fed, a system that dates back to more than a millennium, according to recorded history.

ABOVE Detail of intricate coconut palm-leaf design of a *penjor*.

OPPOSITE *Penjors* line the streets of every village during Galungan. *Penjors* are made by the men of each compound using tall bamboo poles, sheaves of rice, coconuts, foliage and other objects with spiritual meaning. They are placed by the entry gates of each compound along with a shrine. Colourful umbrellas shade the shrines to make an inviting place for ancestors or deities to sit and rest.

This early dried mud and stone wall could be in any one of the Bali Aga villages. However this wall is in the village of Pejeng, in the heart of Gianyar region, where many ancient architectural sites have been located.

BALI AGA VILLAGE CENTRES

Bali Aga people (mountain people) believe they are the original inhabitants of Bali, having lived on the island centuries before the migration of the Majapahit kingdom in the 14th century. They resisted influence from the Majapahit court culture, tenaciously guarding their local laws. By maintaining control of their lands during the expansion of kingdoms, they and their villages have remained independent. As a result, Bali Aga people managed to live close to what is considered their original culture and continue to safeguard that lifestyle.

Practising different forms of Hinduism or Animism, they lived in the more isolated regions of the island. There are several Bali Aga villages, each having a slightly different architectural style. The architecture of Bali Aga villages has a monolithic character, beautifully fundamental with a primitive or ancient feel. Structures do not have the highly decorative details of the more easily recognized Majapahit style. However, certain elements of the Bali Aga style can be seen throughout the island. The villages of Tenganan, Bugbug, Bayung Gede, Trunyan and Penglipuran continue to preserve their architectural tradition of unadorned structures. Structural frameworks are exposed,

regardless of the material (timber, bamboo, stone, mud or thatch) and reveal the honesty in construction techniques. The use of natural, organic materials exemplify the Bali Aga style of architecture.

Tenganan village

Tenganan, near the eastern coastal village of Candi Dasa, is a walled mountain village with distinctive architectural forms. The people of Tenganan believe they are a community of chosen people who have a history that began earlier than the rest of Bali. Stories and old *lontar* manuscripts chronicle legendary tales of the Hindu god Indra founding Tenganan. Not surprisingly, the people have established strict community rules to maintain the purity of bloodlines in honour of their sacred origins. Elegant with a fair complexion and a regal appearance, the people of Tenganan are a relatively well-to-do, land-owning community.

Basket and textile collectors from around the globe make their way to Tenganan village seeking the finely woven baskets made from Ata grass and the complicated textile known as *geringsing*. The women of Tenganan are among the few people in the world who weave this textile.

The stone foundations, thatch and timber of this public pavilion at Tenganan reflect the Bali Aga style of architecture.

Geringsing Geringsing is a double ikat fabric. 'Ikat' means 'to tie', referring to the process of tying bundles of yarn before dyeing (resist dyed) to accomplish different patterning on the individual thread. The warp threads and the weft threads are each dyed with a certain pattern, then woven to achieve complicated floral designs, abstract patterns, images of gods and characters from the *wayang kulit* (shadow puppet) dramas. Colours used are dark rust-brown tones, white and blue-black. Blood is used in the dying process to give the brownish tones. A piece of cloth may take years to weave and is considered to have powerful magical qualities.

OPPOSITE Men of the village of Tenganan are preparing *lawar* (a mixture of pork, coconut, vegetables and spices) for a temple ceremony at the *bale agung*. Tenganan is a walled village with private houses within the interior perimeter of the wall. The village has two main avenues running north to south. Separating the avenues is a series of public pavilions, such as the *bale agung*, used for communal gathering activities.

TOP The entry gate of this home in Tenganan leads into the family shop first and then to the family living area. The variety of materials on its façade—stone, bricks and *popolan*—probably indicates different renovations. The fabrics displayed at the entrance are single ikat and not the sacred *geringsing*.

BOTTOM Even Tenganans cannot resist expressing themselves in this new-style entry gate with magnificent stonework.

PREVIOUS PAGES An impressive *paduraksa*, entry gate of the *pura*, anchors the north end of the main avenue of Penglipuran village. Quiet, calm and tidy... it is an environmentally exceptional atmosphere. The village received awards from the Indonesian government for its standards of beauty, cleanliness and its bamboo forestation programmes.

ABOVE This walled temple in Penglipuran village consists of two long *bale* with raised platforms. The style of *bale* is a split platform pavilion, a monolithic architectural structure of early Bali. The bamboo-shingle roof is host to ferns.

Penglipuran village

The people of Penglipuran village are strongly committed to preserving not only their long-standing *adat* (customary law) but also their system of *ayahan desa*, a philosophy committed to respecting the land of the village. Here is a village that is clean and tidy with great natural beauty. Each afternoon the villagers clean and sweep the main avenue. There is one main avenue running north to south, lined with compound walls interrupted only by entry gates. The few businesses in town are mainly small *warungs* selling coffee and snacks—all concealed within the walls.

Members of the *Desa Adat* (a council that advises on village customary law and culture, similar to a *banjar* organization) play an important role in maintaining the philosophical ideals of this Bali Aga village. A villager, Budi Arta, was strolling the street and wanted to practise his English, and so we chatted a bit. He had been studying English for five years at the University for English Studies in Singaraja and would teach in Denpasar upon completion of his schooling. He said, "There is no caste system here. However, there is a group known as *karma pengarep* who are privileged members, like the original clan [note: original clan refers to the Bali Aga people, the indigenous people of Bali]. Each of them is given an eight-*arah* house yard, 40 *arah* of agricultural land, 70 *arah* of bamboo forest, 60 *arah* of riverside irrigation and 25 *arah* of rice fields (an *arah* is equivalent to 10 square metres). House yards are bordered to the front and sides but open to the rear, and no automobile traffic is allowed on the main avenue. There are distinctive differences in placement of buildings within the compounds at Penglipuran as compared to other villages on Bali: *aling-aling* walls are not used and the kitchens are in a sacred position at the front of the compounds (rather than at the back as in compounds in southern Bali). Kitchens are raised off the ground leaving open space beneath the kitchen floors for storage; there is barely room to stand as the ceilings are very low, and there is always a place for sleeping (really just a mattress to one side on the wood floor). People may not sell their land without approval of the villagers and the *Desa Adat* committee. We want to preserve our village, our bamboo forests and our way of life."

Budi walked us to his father's sacred bamboo garden. On Bali, bamboo forests are cool, dark, magical places treated with reverence and respect. The Balinese believe bamboo has qualities of magic and it is certainly true that bamboo has extraordinary characteristics. In fact, without bamboo, the culture of Bali—especially the architecture—would be quite different. Someone once counted the many practical uses of bamboo and the different ways bamboo is used in making various products; there were more than 1500 examples when they stopped counting. Here in Penglipuran village, 15 types of bamboo are grown and selectively harvested once a year. *Tiying selem* is a strikingly handsome black bamboo; *tiying ampel* is used as rafters in roofing or in products that are woven; *tiying tali* is a rope made from bamboo; and *tiying jajang* is for house construction because of its larger diameter.

We were indeed enchanted, just walking along the winding paths through the forest, listening to the wind sing through waving stalks of bamboo as the golden light of the afternoon sun played on the tall, arching shafts. Emerging from the bamboo grove, Budi led the way to his father's large garden with many fruiting trees and small crops of maize, aubergine and beans. On that day they were harvesting cocoa.

EBF The Environmental Bamboo Foundation (EBF) in cooperation with Penglipuran village set up a training centre on village lands to promote bamboo preservation. A grant from USAID and Earth Love (UK) helped finance the purchase of basic tools and machines for making ply-bamboo. The villagers in turn contribute land and labour for construction and manage the project together with the EBF. Founded in 1993 by Linda Garland, an Australian living in Bali, its mission is to protect tropical forests by promoting the many environmental and economic opportunities that bamboo offers. Bamboo is now on Indonesia's conservation and development agenda.

Green cocoa fruit grow directly out of trunks of the cacao tree, as do jackfruit and other exotic fruits on Bali.

Cocoa is a good cash crop for this villager. The fruit is spread out to dry in the sun; its white fibres wither away leaving the cocoa bean to be sold for processing.

LEFT *Pemangku* Jero Kubayan, wearing a *poleng* waist cloth, joins villagers in a *bale* for an afternoon chat. This four-posted *bale* is completely traditional in scale and design. The roofing is made of bamboo shingles.

Bugbug village

Bugbug is a coastal village in eastern Bali in the Karangasam region. The architecture here is far different from both Tenganan and Penglipuran villages. The village consists of a series of narrow alleyways bordered by stone walls of individual compounds. Tiny entry gates are the only relief from the long hall-like paths. Narrow alleyways open onto the central square of the village. The square runs east to west with shops to the south and a large communal *bale agung* and temple to the north.

BOTTOM Along a coastal road near Bugbug, palm fronds are set out to dry for use as firewood and fencing. The *alang-alang* roof seen just beyond the fence has split coconuts stacked one on another as the decorative 'hat' for the roof.

RIGHT Stone-walled alleyways open onto the village square at one end and to a back roadway at the other. The strong monolithic design gives the village the feel of an ancient society. Tiled roofs and electricity wires are concessions to modern life.

FAMILY COMPOUNDS

Bunuton village

The compounds of different villages may vary in style and layout but they are generally walled gardens with a series of *bale* and enclosed rooms for sleeping, called *bale meten*. The tidy village of Bunuton, north of Ubud, is very much like many other villages in the south of Bali where residents busily combine their daily work with endless social responsibilities of the *banjar*, countless preparations for the perpetual round of temple celebrations and ceremonies along with obligations to the family and extended family. Anthropologist Margaret Mead wrote in the 1930s, after extensive research on the Balinese personality: "there is an incredible busyness on Bali". The constant busyness is one very remarkable aspect of daily life on Bali and we chose to photograph two of Bunuton's walled family compounds to illustrate the way families live 'at home'.

ABOVE Sculpture and lush plants create an inviting entry garden in a family compound in Bunuton. The arched, thatched roof of a rice granary, the *lumbung*, can be seen towards the back.

RIGHT The garden courtyard of this compound in Bunuton is swept early in the morning and several times each day to keep a tidy appearance. Gardens in compounds are usually planted with flowering trees and fruit trees.

LEFT Entry gate to the compound of a family of stone carvers and painters in Bunuton. The gate has traditional proportions with a series of modernized Boma (man of the forest) images over the door rather than the usual single image. A playful Balinese girl—standing between a just-as-playful stone couple—waits to greet us.

ABOVE This *bale meten*—with its ceramic tiled floors, brick or concrete block construction and tiled roof—is a typical style on modern Bali. Still, some basic elements of traditional architecture are used; these can be seen in the proportions of the structure, in the posts that stand on bollard and in the carved double entry door. The floor is elevated about 40 centimetres off the ground to facilitate sitting on the edge of the verandah. A very attractive air-vent design has been incorporated into the end wall.

ABOVE Agama-Hindu requires abundant quantities of offerings. The art of making offerings—with their complicated designs, nuances attached to ingredients, colour requirements and the understanding of the calendar of events—is a lesson learned from mothers and grandmothers.

LEFT A colourful *lumbung* in a compound in Bunuton. The roof was probably made of *alang-alang* thatch at one time but economic pressures and availability of cheaper materials make corrugated steel the material of choice.

RIGHT *Bale dangin*, the honoured pavilion in a compound, is the place for family ceremonies as well as the sleeping place for grandparents. This pavilion has fine carvings above the sleeping platform, including a carved roof support in the shape of the mythical Garuda bird. The women are dressed in traditional *kebaya* and sarong to make offerings.

COMPOUND SEDERHANA

Sederhana literally means 'plain' or 'simple' and is the descriptive word for a modest compound of *sudra* (common people) families. All of the components that can be found in traditional, residential architecture are used here: a wall surrounds the compound, there is an entry gate with *aling-aling*, and the style and placement of *bale* within the compound walls are the same. But there is a simplicity of design and the use of readily available materials lends a completely organic atmosphere. Compound *sederhana* can be found all over Bali but are usually found in more rural districts away from tourist centres. Sometimes, a compound *sederhana* with a simple *popolan* (adobe) entry gate may be located just next door to a Majapahit-style gate with carvings and complicated brick work; the contrast of primitive design and the highly embellished style is always a delight to the eye.

OPPOSITE TOP The entry gate structure in this compound *sederhana* in Jukut Paku, Singakerta, shows signs of giving way. Fresh offerings have been placed in the niches of this *batu paras* (sandstone) gate. The *aling-aling* beyond is made of concrete blocks.

OPPOSITE BOTTOM A farmer heads home after a day at work.

TOP This compound in the village of Batuan on the road between Denpasar and Ubud has pavilions constructed of *popolan*. Deterioration of the adobe shows *bata citakan* (mud bricks) or *bata bola* (mud balls) used as a substrate. The cobbled pavement of the courtyard is an upgrade from bare earth, which is usually seen in traditional compound *sederhana*. Bamboo poles help support the ageing roof structure.

BOTTOM This *bale meten* (closed pavilion for sleeping) is made of *popolan*, as are houses and walls found in modest compounds throughout rural Bali.

ABOVE Honeymoon Guest House showcases an exciting combination of traditional roof designs utilizing tiles, thatched roofs of *alang-alang* and ironwood shingles on the many different pavilions in the compound.

OPPOSITE Woodcarving on the entry gate is by Ketut Suardana's woodcarving studio. This gate is used by guests at the homestay or at the restaurant that can be seen just beyond the *palimanan* stone statue of the elephant god Ganesha.

BALINESE BED AND BREAKFAST — THE *LOSMAN*

Losman are small homestays, the Balinese version of bed and breakfast accommodation. Amenities include wake-up calls by a resident rooster, night-time music by a chorale of frogs in nearby rice fields and the pleasure of watching and participating in the daily activities of a Balinese family. Western tourists seeking a cultural experience of living with and getting to know a native family choose to stay in a *losman* as these buildings are actually part of a typical family compound. They are usually one-storey bungalows with an open verandah, very much like the traditional *bale meten*. Rooms have bare minimum furnishings but are comfortable and clean as can be. Breakfast is most likely delicately-thin banana crepes, fresh fruit salad and Bali *kopi*; all these are included in the price of the room and served on the verandah by a friendly, smiling, ready-to-chat family member.

The Honeymoon Guest House is a typical *losman* and then more. The buildings are a study of all the classic elements of Balinese architecture, charmingly placed in gardens of shrubs and flowering trees with winding paths flowing throughout the grounds. Rooms are elegant with carved teak and mahogany furniture from Indonesia. Then just next door is the Honeymoon Bakery, where the aroma of freshly baked breakfast rolls and pastries rouses all sleepy heads out of their comfy beds to have breakfast served on the verandah of their rooms.

This up-scale *losman* is located just west of Ubud, up a bumpy cobbled-stone lane to the compound of Ketut Suardana and Janet deNeefe. Janet is from Australia, Ketut is from Ubud and they share their home with their four young children. Their compound is a busy place with the comings and goings of the many family members, friends of the community and staff of the couple's multiple business ventures, which includes Casa Luna Restaurant, Indus Restaurant and Honeymoon Bakery. Then there are also the guests at the homestay and the students who attend Janet's cooking school. Both Janet and Ketut are entrepreneurs but "Ketut on a grander scale than me," says Janet. They see the restaurants and their other businesses as an educational opportunity for the local employees—they have seen their employees' housing improve and hope their lives are also improving.

The compound is a combination of traditions. Certainly the architectural style is Balinese but since both Janet and Ketut feel a need to bring the outside in, their private home is modified to satisfy Janet's concepts of a comfortable home. At the front of the compound, just inside the highly carved *kori* entry gate is the traditional family temple placed in the honoured northeastern corner. Prominently placed in the centre of the family courtyard is the *bale dangin*, a pavilion used for traditional ceremonies celebrated throughout the Agama-Hindu calendar year for important rituals. The *bale dangin* was used for ceremonies that were held when their children were born, and will be used for tooth filings, marriage ceremonies when the time comes and for other rituals. Gold-leafed and polychromed carvings on the *bale dangin* were produced by Ketut's woodcarving studio, the Pantheon Gallery, in the village of Mas.

Their home is decorated with traditional carvings and motifs inspired by the Majapahit period of architecture, but it is not traditional in layout or in height as it has two storeys (the Balinese prefer sleeping on the ground floor). Rather than a separate building for the kitchen, there is a 'great-room' with dining and cooking as part of the main house. Janet needed and insisted the kitchen be inside the house, much to the consternation of the village workers who helped build the house. The frontispiece of Janet's cookbook *Fragrant Rice* reads: "My continuing love affair with Bali. A tale of passion, marriage and food." This book is her own memoir paired with her favourite Balinese recipes. Her restaurants were among the first in Ubud to offer a varied menu of local foods along with other dishes tasty to westerners. She begins the first chapter with this quote:

They looked like an ocean of blossoming flowers
In their brilliant festival attire,
And it was especially the lovely women who created
This beautiful scene,
With the movement of their eyebrows as sharp
as slivers of gravel.

— Parthayana, The Journeying of Partha

Janet has embraced the Balinese way of life but has also integrated her own style of living, having grown up in Australia. Janet and Ketut's love affair, their darling children and the home they have created, as well as their public lives in Ubud are exemplary.

Entry hall of the family home has a Western-influenced stairway to the master bedroom. The pavilion straight ahead is the children's wing. Art deco-style chair is made on Bali. Teak entry table, mirror and accessories are from Java.

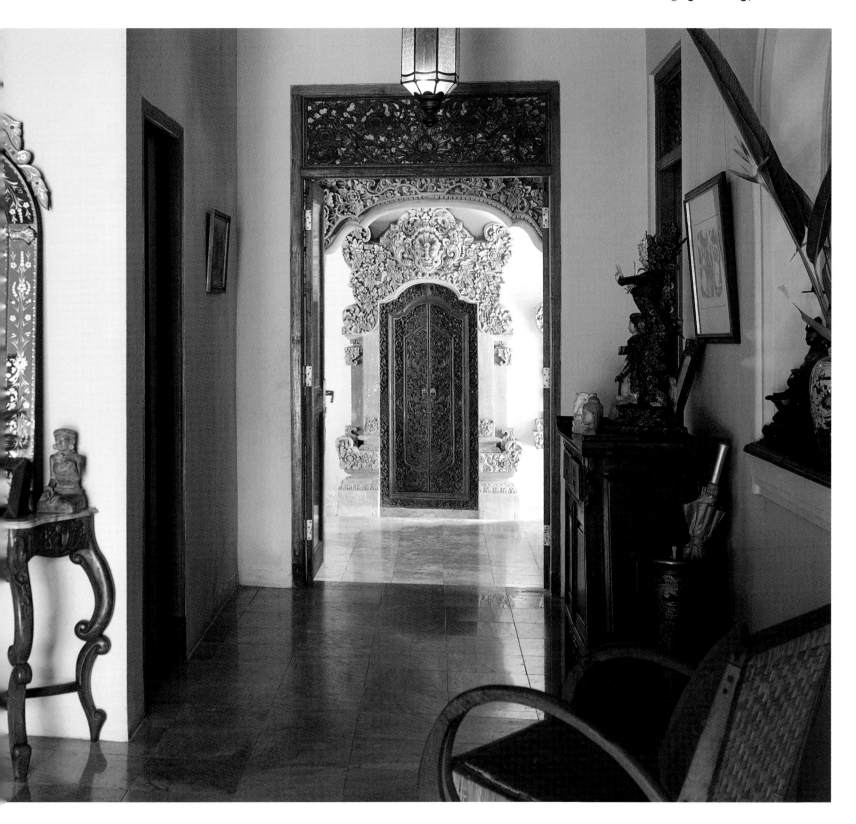

LEFT This is the courtyard gathering place of the family home. The *bale* in the foreground is for family and friends to gather and socialize, and the place for Janet's cooking school lessons which she conducts a few times each week. The highly carved *bale* with gold-leaf is the *bale dangin*, the place for religious ceremonies. Ketut is on the verandah, enjoying his usual morning ritual of reading the *Bali Post* while sipping a dark brew of Bali *kopi* before he begins his day.

ABOVE This extraordinary *kori* is entry to the family compound but guests are invited to enter here as well. It was designed by Ketut Suardana and executed on the site. The gilded doors were carved at his woodcarving studio.

Through the open windows of the family living room, one gets a stunning view of the well-crafted gold-leaf carvings on the back wall of the *bale dangin*. Janet is seen teaching a cooking class to students in the front *bale*.

Vibrant green kitchen cabinets make a joyful place to
try new dishes for the family and restaurant menus.
Colourful Indonesian fabrics cover pillows on teak
benches at the family dining table. Open panels
in transoms of windows allow ventilation when the
louvred shutters are closed.

COMPOUND HOUSE — VILLAGE HOME ADAPTED

In the extraordinary home of Sana Hiromi and Made Sudiana Bendesa, a harmonious melding of two distinct cultures has produced a phenomenal adaptation. The way to this remarkable house located beyond the village of Mas is through small hamlets where newly harvested rice piled on red plastic tarpaulins and left to dry on roadways in the sun are a common sight.

Turning on to a narrower road there are small groups of men sitting on their haunches exercising their fighting cocks.

Twisting and turning, the roads continue on through slightly terraced *sawah* (rice fields) and then in the distance, a group of dark tiled roofs makes an appearance in the midst of endless green rice fields. On closer approach, the roofs belong to long, low houses that are carefully positioned and artfully lost in the magnificent emerald ocean of *sawah*.

The entry drive to this compound of houses is bordered on each side by curving walls built with stacked river stone in dark grey and black tones. The rock wall undulates and curves, raising one's anticipation to see full on the cluster of houses. The first house is the home of a friend from Japan; the next is where Made Sudiana's mother lives; and just next

OPPOSITE Round, stacked river rocks form a curving entry to the Sana-Bendesa home. The driveway is loose gravel and scored concrete.

ABOVE Slight terracing of the front yard is a memory of the old *sawah* field where this home now stands. The low window is at floor level inside the entry foyer, attractive from inside and a handsome element in a large exterior wall.

These magnificent entry doors are framed by strong teak columns and *merbau*-wood cross beams. The glass above the doors gives a sneak preview of the exciting ceiling of the interior, which extends to the eaves on the exterior.

to this house is the main house, the remarkable fine home of Sana Hiromi and her husband Made Sudiana Bendesa. Sana Hiromi is from Japan and Made Sudiana is a well-known woodcarver from the Balinese village of Mas. After many years of marriage, Hiromi and Made Sudiana chose to build a home that would be a coming together of the cultural heritages of both Japan and Bali.

The combined artistic vision of this highly accomplished couple has resulted in a home that is not only well proportioned, aesthetically pleasing and imaginative in the details but one that has also met the requirements of two distinct cultures. Made Sudiana relates funny stories of the design-and-build process involving the house's two designers—the married homeowners themselves. They discussed the design in Japanese, Bahasa

This raised gathering place is the sacred centre and nucleus of the home.
The floor is made from *kelakala* wood from the Celebes islands. The ceiling is
graced with an ancient, carved-wood, tiered ceiling from the old Parliament
house in Mataram, Java. The posts extend from the ceilings down through the
low wall of stone tiles to the floor, a true expression of authentic design and
truth in materials.

Indonesia and Bahasa Bali, each believing they had clearly communicated their personal vision of details to the other. When asked if there were working drawings, Made Sudiana said, "Yes, one sheet of paper that is rubbed through with erasing and completely marked-up with changes."

The house grew and developed from an overriding principle of a sacred centre: a house with a mid-point, a centre for gathering, a place of prominence in the living area of the home. This gathering place would provide a nucleus for the coming together of diverse people; it would be a place where guests, family, friends and business acquaintances could come together for the exchange, communication and blending of ideas.

An ancient carved wood ceiling, a *joglo*, from the Parliament House in Mataram, Java, sits above this central gathering place. The ceiling borrows its form from the pagoda-shaped *meru* in that it has an uneven number of levels that diminish in size from bottom to top. The carvings on this 9-tiered ceiling are a blend of sacred Hindu motifs from India and the Majapahit era of Java. Made Sudiana says, "I feel it is important to make continuous history from India to Java to Bali. Bali is the flower of Java." Hiromi and Made Sudiana believe the tiered shape of the ceiling directs God's spiritual energy to the gathering beneath. This divine energy strengthens those who have come to share ideas and creates communication that is more humane.

Detail of the ironwood, 9-tiered ceiling from Mataram that lies strategically over the heart of the family gathering place. The carvings on each tier have a specific meaning. Note the main ceiling of the house—the *merbau* cross beams and rafters are attached using traditional tongue and groove joinery; the ceiling forms an exciting backdrop for this free-floating, antique *joglo* centrepiece.

Made Sudiana feels that a place for human communication must be constructed from wood, which he speaks of from a reverent perspective:

"My life is totally about wood, from wood. My village of Mas is about wood. Seven hundred years before the Majapahit kingdom came to Bali (perhaps about AD 600 to AD 800), a priest, Pedanda Sakti Wawurauh, travelled around Bali, then chose to stay in Mas. He stuck his walking stick into the ground and it hidup *(lived, took root), growing into a tree that flowered big, gold flowers. Pedanda Wawurauh proclaimed the ground and area clean (sacred), named the area Mas, and said the people of Mas should make their life from wood. That is the philosophy of Mas village and explains why it is a village of woodcarvers."*

Sana Hiromi completed this story by saying the Japanese and Balinese cultures share the same belief regarding the sacredness of wood. She herself is the granddaughter of a carpenter. Therefore, their children inherit an ancestry of woodworkers from both their mother and father.

On the use of wood for their distinctive gathering place, a sacred centre, the couple chose to use *kelakala* wood from the Celebes islands for its floor. This platform in turn is raised from the main living area to become an inviting stage with floor pillows and a naturally planed teak table from Made Sudiana's production studio. The day I visited this space, green Japanese tea was ceremoniously served while the children of the house were happily playing in the lawn between the gathering place and the *sawah*. Made Sudiana later opened a young coconut, slivered the soft, translucent white flesh and placed it on a Japanese tray along with bright mango slices. Using chopsticks we dipped these delicacies into a special soya sauce from Japan and relished the cool and unusual combination of tastes. Certainly a transition from the mundane was made while sitting under that carved wood ceiling as we shared concepts, ideas and exotic tastes from a wide world of choices. On this day, Made Sudiana's theories of why conversation areas must be made of wood were proven correct.

The dramatic design features of this exceptional house include large-diameter teak logs used as posts and crossbeams of *merbau* wood from Irian Jaya. Tongue and groove joinery eliminates a need for nails. The ceiling is made from woven bamboo matting with rafters of *merbau* wood. All of the woodwork details are designed by Made Sudiana and Hiromi and accomplished either on site or at one of Made Sudiana's woodworking studios or factory. Kitchen cabinets are made from dense *tagaya* wood from Japan.

The large double entry doors are a combination of teak, ebony and wrought metal with a special hinge detail designed by Made Sudiana. The floor hinge was executed in ebony wood with stainless steel ball bearings (see detail drawing in the Architectural Notebook). The entry steps are made from

OPPOSITE The large custom-made *merbau*-wood doors pivot on offset hinges so that they may swing either way. Carvings around the family pavilion door are from the workshops of Made Sudiana. The pavilion beyond is the family library and the children's rooms. Upstairs and accessed by a stairway in the family library is the master bedroom.

ABOVE Detail of a three-dimensional woodcarving by the studios of Made Sudiana. The carving is of a dragon swimming among the waves of a sea. This extraordinary carving is made from petrified *jindai keyaki* wood from Japan. Hiromi and Made Sudiana tell a story of noises keeping them awake at night after the completion of some renovation work. Made Sudiana's father reminded them they had not done the completion ceremonies and therefore, the tail of the dragon was slapping back and forth and not at rest. They called a priest and performed all of the necessary ceremonies and no longer heard noises in the night.

dark granite from Java. Window details follow traditional Japanese design to allow controlled cross-ventilation and the windowsills are teak with edges left unworked to express the natural, irregular shape of the wood.

Balinese houses do not typically have basements or crawl spaces. However there is an area beneath this house filled with dry coral rock, gathered from a hill near Ulu Watu, topped by layers of charcoal made from bamboo. The charcoal helps to filter the air and air vents strategically placed around the perimeter walls of the foundation area ensure a flow of filtered air. The front door of the house is oriented to the East, allowing the morning sun to bathe the entrance and kitchen. Made Sudiana says with a smile, "It is a very nice feeling to open the front door and have the East before you. The entry doors open inward allowing the energy of the East to flow into the house—Balinese feng shui."

This house of exceptional design, detail, style and elegance is the result of the considerable imagination and talent of artists Sana Hiromi and Made Sudiana Bendesa. Here is a fine example of blending cultural ideals in architectural detailing to accomplish a home that is a work of art.

TOP The family dining area has another Made Sudiana table made from natural teak. Edges and imperfections of the wood are left as they are; a deep cleft in the tabletop is filled with tiny black pebbles. The kitchen area steps down and cabinets are designed to accommodate the proportions of the main cook, Sana Hiromi.

BOTTOM The bedroom of the owners' two sons is a tatami-sized room with sliding shoji screen doors. Base of beds is natural teak (2 metres by 1.5 metres and 10 centimetres thick). The view from the room is to the green rice fields that surround the house.

ABOVE The large tables are natural teak slabs from Made Sudiana's workshop. The mandalas were designed and painted for a temple in Japan by Sana Hiromi's fine art workshop. Also designed by Hiromi is the hand-painted silk runner on the dining table depicting a landscape and flowing river before the sun comes up. Hiromi explains the subject, Change of Tides: "At the point where river meets sea, there is a change of movement, like our lives flowing, meeting resistance and then changing." The wood sculpture on the table is of a Balinese woman bathing in a river; the base is carved to resemble water. The sculpture and silk runner are intertwined with meanings. The sculpture standing by the mandala is Dewi Sri, the rice goddess. All sculptures and woodcarvings, including the table base and door transom, are made by Made Sudiana's workshops. The painting on the far wall is by friend and well-known painter Arie Smit.

LEFT Detail of teak columns and *merbau* cross beams and rafters. Small rocks set into the jambs of the door and window add another organic material to the mix. The musical instrument is from a bamboo gamelan, the *angklung*, and the painting is also by Arie Smit.

OPPOSITE Back view of the house showing a deck off the interior gathering place platform. Post-and-beam structure is exposed throughout the entire house. The upper balcony of the two-storey pavilion belongs to the master bedroom.

LEFT A room with a fantastic view—the master bedroom suite of Hiromi and Made Sudiana. The ceiling is warm and textural with rattan matting and *merbau* wood rafters. Mosquito netting is by I. Wirata's Sama Sama Shop in Campuhan.

THE PURI AGUNG UBUD

We entered the courtyard of Puri Agung Ubud; there was an expectant audience settled for an evening performance. The spicy smell of clove cigarettes mingled in the heavy night air with the fragrance of frangipani and burning incense. A Balinese man entered from one side, barefoot and dressed in a sarong. He lighted a torch and began to climb to the top of the high kori agung *gate. He lighted little coconut oil lanterns as he descended, each little light flickering against the deep carvings of the stone. A* pemangku, *dressed all in white put down offerings, rang his tinkling bell and offered prayers. The gamelan orchestra sat on the ground behind their instruments, each wearing a sarong, a jacket the colour of red ginger and a white head band. The deep baritone of the gong* gede *sounded —followed by the crashing melodious sounds of gamelan* legong, *sending a primal note of remembrance through my body. Pendet dancers entered and showered a welcome of fresh blossoms on the silent audience. We were completely enchanted.*

— Journal entry from *Between Night and Day in Bali*, 7 January 1988, by Barbara Walker

LEFT Ancar Saji courtyard of Puri Agung Ubud. Architect I. Gusti Lempad designed the restoration of the Majapahit-style gate after a destructive earthquake in 1917 damaged the original gate. This ornately carved gate provides a stage and backdrop for evening performances of traditional Balinese dance. The *puri* is a nightly gathering place in Ubud where tourists and locals assemble to watch quality traditional performances. A superb gamelan orchestra and talented dancers make an evening at the *puri* a memorable experience. There is an impact on the senses by the vivid imagery of dancers in brilliant coloured, bejewelled costumes adorned with fresh flowers, their movements intensified by the crescendo and complex sounds of the gamelan orchestra.

The Puri Agung Ubud (Royal Palace of Ubud) is the centre of Ubud in many ways. Even literally speaking, the palace is located at the centre of the village at the crossroads of Jalan Raya and Jalan Monkey Forest, across from the *pasar*, or market. More importantly, however, is how the Royal Family stands central to Ubud's artistic, economic and social life. Puri Agung Ubud has had the interest of the village at heart for more than 150 years and remains a tireless patron of its cultural endeavours.

Bali's kingdoms warred and exchanged territories many times in the written history of Bali, but it was from the 17th to the 19th centuries that the royal houses of the greater Ubud area actually emerged from a multitude of small kingdoms. A new period of prosperity began for the Ubud area during the reign of Tjokorde Rai Batur, from 1850 to 1880. Tjokorde Rai was a spiritual man with little interest in militant activities with the other kingdoms or with the Dutch colonialists and he may have set a tone that was followed by subsequent *tjokorde* of Puri Agung Ubud. However, the next raja, Tjokorde Gede Sukawati (1880–1917), was forced to take up arms once again in neighbouring districts and for the last time in modern history. Tjokorde Gede Sukawati's *kris* (ceremonial knife with a wavy blade) had special powers of creating an illusion that caused the enemy to believe they were seeing more opposing soldiers than were actually there and so to flee the scene of battle. The power of his *kris* was legendary.

Until the *Puputan* (suicidal fight to death when defeat is inevitable) of 1906, when some royal families turned their *kris* upon themselves rather than submit to the Dutch, Bali was a place of unrest and political conflict. Following this episode, world opinion forced the Dutch to reconsider how to administer authority over Bali and they established new rules to help preserve the cultural identity of the Balinese. These rules gave Bali a greater independence than other Indonesian islands, an important decision that played a role in preserving the traditional Balinese culture.

In 1910, Ubud's next raja, Tjokorde Gede Agung Sukawati, the son of Tjokorde Gede Sukawati, was born. As a young man he left Ubud to live with an elder brother at the Puri Belaluan in Denpasar, which was located across the street from the Dutch-run Bali Hotel. He decided to quit school at the age of 15 to become a tour guide for guests at the Bali Hotel. He quickly learned Dutch and English from the visitors. By the age of 17, he had married his first wife (the first of eleven). At this point he moved back to Ubud and began a small guesthouse in the Puri Agung Ubud.

Historically, Ubud was well known to the Balinese as a healthy place to live, not only because of its cooler air but also because it was a place to seek out medical advice from local healers, the *balian*. From the time of Rsi Markandeya's pilgrimage to the nearby village of Campuhan in AD 800, Ubud was known as a centre of great spiritual power and energy. In the early 20th century when the Dutch began to promote Bali as a tourist destination, Ubud was the hands-down favourite spot. Adrian Vickers writes in his book, *Bali: A Paradise Created*, of a tourist brochure issued in 1914 by the Dutch:

> "Bali—you leave the island with a sigh of regret and as long as you live you can never forget this garden of Eden."

And so in 1927 when Tjokorde Gede Agung Sukawati returned to Ubud from Denpasar, it was a time when Bali was becoming a stop on the world tours of travellers in the know. He invited Walter Spies, a musician from Germany who had been living in the Royal Kraton (palace) in Yogyakarta, Java, to visit Ubud. Both men formed a great friendship resulting in the *tjokorde* offering him a site in Campuhan to build a house. The talents of the charming Walter Spies—he was also a fine artist—combined with the social graces and power of Tjokorde Gede Agung Sukawati formed a catalyst that began the remarkable period of intellectual and artistic endeavour on Bali in the 1930s.

Until this time the artisans of Bali worked mainly under the guidance of the royal families, painting or carving subjects of a religious nature or the mythological characters of the *Mahabharata* and *Ramayana* epics. Puri Agung Ubud, under the kingship of Tjokorde Gede Agung Sukawati, relaxed the traditional artistic rules, allowing artists to not only change the subjects of works but also to mix and experiment with new colours that were previously not allowed. Without the Palace's support, these changes would not have occurred at that time.

Tjokorde Gede Agung Sukawati, Gusti Nyoman Lempad (painter, sculptor and architect), Walter Spies, Rudolph Bonnet (an important Western artist of this period) and Anak Agung Gede Sobrat furthered the role of Ubud in the world of fine art by forming an organization for painters called the Pita Maha group. The Pita Maha, which means 'guiding spirit or great shining', group was a cooperative of artists and art dealers set up with the purpose of stimulating the arts. This organization, along with celebrated writers, helped create the perception of Ubud as *the* centre for performance art and fine art. The Puri Lukisan Museum was built on palace grounds to exhibit Balinese paintings, another step by this early group in the promotion of Ubud and Balinese art.

Following the miseries of the Japanese Occupation during World War II and Indonesia's fight for independence against the Dutch, the years between 1940 and the 1960s were a time of turmoil and struggle. Nevertheless, Tjokorde Gede Agung continued to entertain celebrities and notables during these years: Robert F. Kennedy, then U.S. attorney general; Queen Juliana of the Netherlands; and Jawaharlal Nehru of India are a few of the heads of state to visit Bali. In the 1970s, artistic and academic types began to return to rural and quiet Bali. They found a community in Ubud to explore their art and opportunities to study with talented people. The royal family encouraged this development with their considerable wealth and support.

RIGHT This *bale ageng* is reserved for the royal family's rites-of-passage ceremonies. The four stones to the left of the steps mark the site of a childbirth ritual that took place at the birth of each of the four children of Raja Tjokorde Gede Agung Sukawati. An Agama-Hindu traditional ceremony requires the placenta, umbilical cord and some amniotic fluid to be placed in a young, yellow coconut. The coconut is then wrapped in sugar-palm fibre and buried in the family courtyard. The Barong puppet used for dance performances is honourably stored in this *bale*. Artworks by local painters and sculptors are temporarily on display here as they were under consideration for the Puri Lukisan Museum the day we took this photograph.

ABOVE Puri Agung Ubud is home to the Royal Family of Ubud. Carved wood covered in gold-leaf combined with *batu bali* (the red bricks of Bali) and carved *batu paras* makes an elegant setting for meetings and social events. Tjokorde Gede Putra Sukawati (extreme right) spends much time meeting with local community leaders, heads of state from foreign countries and Indonesian officials.

OPPOSITE TOP The Trompong dance is a spectacle at the Puri Agung Ubud. Flashing hands and eyes and quick elegant movements, complemented by a glittering gold costume, are all punctuated with the syncopated percussion rhythms of the gamelan orchestra.

OPPOSITE BOTTOM The exciting Baris with ceremonial *kris* strapped to his back demonstrates through dance a full range of emotions befitting a warrior; fierceness, strength, dignity and also tenderness. This solo performance for young male dancers is held at the Ancar Saji courtyard of Puri Agung Ubud.

Tjokorde Gede Agung's royal cremation in 1979 began a new period of responsibility and devotion to Ubud by his three sons, the princes of Ubud. Tjokorde Gede Putra Sukawati, the eldest son, assumed the role of leader for the royal family. He remains untiring in his determination to support the ideals set forth by his father while meeting the challenges of a modern Bali. Together with his brothers, architect Tjokorde Gede Oka and Tjokorde Gede Raka, they share the responsibilities of operating the family businesses. Their sister, Tjokorde Istri Atun Sukawati, lives in Denpasar.

Today, the royal palace's outer courtyard provides an elegant gathering place for nightly performances of traditional dances not only for the benefit of showcasing the talent of local artists but also for tourists to see Balinese performances. Ubud has become a town of festivals, such as the annual Ubud Writers and Readers Festival or the Conference for World Peace and Healing, and the Palace is a supporter of this type of activity. Tjokorde Gede Putra acts as the advisor to the chairman of the Bali Tourism Board and heads committees on the beautification of Ubud.

The royal family also continues to operate Hotel Tjampuhan, the oldest and most traditional hotel in Ubud, as well as three other hotel properties. The princes are completely involved in the welfare of Ubud, supporting tourism activities and are an active force determined to continue Bali's cultural heritage. As Tjokorde Gede Putra Sukawati says: "It is important to preserve Ubud in each period. It was unique in the 1930s, the 1950s and now we face new challenges, but will strive to continue the unique and special qualities of Ubud. We do not want to block change, but combine changes that conform with the ideals of *adat* and *budaya*. It is important to share the spirit of Bali, the spirit of communally shared life as expressed in the village."

The royal family offers their home, the Puri Agung Ubud, as a gathering place for people to discuss and resolve political and social affairs and to engage in their artistic pursuits. Puri Agung Ubud is a gathering place not only for the Balinese, but also for visitors because it is a place where they can learn more about the Balinese culture.

OPPOSITE This entry gate leading to private quarters was designed by I. Gusti Lempad in 1917. The *aling-aling* wall is a traditional element in temples, village compounds and here at the Palace. A water garden has been added to the courtyard side of the *aling-aling*.

LEFT This gate leading into the staff quarters is of a very different style. Built in the early 20th century and also designed by I. Gusti Lempad, it appears to have an art nouveau influence.

The auspicious day for the cremation has arrived and last minute touches are being made to the sarcophagus. The *lembu* (bull or cow) sarcophagus represents a vehicle of Siwa—that aspect of god that symbolizes death and destruction but happily the recycling of spiritual life. Large ramp to the *bade* allows the body to be placed in the tower. A similar ramp has been built at the cemetery to remove the body from the tower and then placed in the sarcophagus for cremation. A statue of the Monkey-General, Hanuman, is on guard at the ramp.

A Royal Cremation

Cremations in Bali are usually colourful ceremonies with much commotion and gaiety. Upon the death of the twin sister of Raja Tjokorde Gede Agung Sukawati, the Balinese royal family staged a glorious extravaganza that was all gold, glittering and astonishing—some say as impressive as the one held when the Raja died in 1979. The community effort required to plan and flawlessly present this elaborate ceremony provides insight into the social strength of the Balinese cultural system.

For more than one month before the auspicious day for the cremation ceremony, called a *palebon* in the high language used for royalty (called *nygben* for the cremation of a lower caste person), the street beside the royal palace in Ubud was crowded with construction and closed to traffic. Preparation for the royal *palebon* involved the members of more than five adjoining villages. Ubud was positively swarming with activity. The preparations involved constructing a tall tower known as *bade*, which is used to ceremoniously carry the body to the cemetery for cremation. The *bade* for this royal *palebon* was 25 metres high and made of large-diameter bamboo. Our photographs show only a few of the other structures constructed although there were hundreds of modestly constructed offerings of fresh flowers, palm fronds, coloured rice dough, spirit houses, roasted pigs and ducks with fabric-draped bamboo poles everywhere. Miraculously all preparations were complete on the day of the ceremony; even electricity and telephone wires were taken down to allow the tall tower to pass. Thousands gathered for the 2-kilometre procession down Jalan Raya Ubud to the cemetery.

A bamboo platform large enough to accommodate 100 men was constructed beneath the main tower. At the appointed moment, the first group of men arrived. As the huge gong and percussion instruments of the *bleganjur gamelan* orchestra struck an earth shattering volume of syncopated rhythm, the men heaved the tower above their heads with a huge roar. Every few metres saw the exchange of another crew of 100 men since the weight of the tower was extreme. Before

A 25-metre tower composed of large-diameter bamboo is under construction in the street beside the palace. Villagers from five *banjars* helped in preparations for the cremation and to build this *bade*.

A *pedanda*, or high priest, offers prayers before the *palebon* ceremonies begin.

the ceremony, the men went early to the temple and prayed for the spirits to enter their bodies and give them the strength to carry the *bade*.

Streets were jammed; it was difficult to imagine how one person could move through the crowd, much less a large moving object. Somehow, as the large structures began the procession to the cemetery, all bystanders fell in behind the main procession without incident or crowd-control barriers. With the explosive sounds of gongs, drums and cymbals, a true festival atmosphere prevailed. Clever sarong sellers, with tall bundles of sarongs balanced on their heads, took advantage of

a day when everyone must wear a sarong. Lingering above all the commotion was the scent of sandalwood incense mingling with the aroma of roast suckling pig offerings.

Balinese ceremonial structures and offerings are made with loving devotion to their culture and the continuation of Balinese traditions. Without much concern for today or tomorrow, the Balinese create transitory art masterpieces not just for this royal funeral but in their everyday lives on a constantly revolving schedule of rituals. Their creativity and their willingness to be completely engaged in their cultural heritage supports the *budaya* of Bali.

Gathering places for tamu

PRIVATE HOUSES

Tamu... this is the affectionate name the Balinese have given to people from other places. Bali is a place where you are made to feel welcomed, as if your arrival has been anticipated and everyone is happy that you have come. You are greeted by name and quickly become part of a community. All know where you come from and how long you plan to stay, and if you are married, how many children you have. The Balinese are friendly; they love to question and answer questions, and they like to joke, sometimes sounding a bit ribald for Western ears. They seem to never forget a face or the details of one's life. They have had a century of experience with *tamu* and appear to be happy with tourism in general; they feel their lives are better in most ways because of the foreigners.

Tourism is not new to Bali; in fact, it was encouraged by the Dutch during their colonial occupation in an attempt to make the island more profitable. By the 1930s Bali had become a stopover on the world tour of the rich and famous, Hollywood movie stars, as well as researchers from every academic field who came to survey the environment and culture. Visitors arrived mostly from Europe to learn first-hand about the 'utopian paradise' of Bali. Among them were Miguel Covarrubias and his wife Rose who visited the island during a world tour that

Cooking lessons at Laka Leke with master chef Ibu Wayan are a time for learning about new ingredients, new seasonings and special techniques for slicing and dicing. Near the cooking *bale* are beds of organic herbs and local vegetables for students to pick for the class.

From the bluffs of Jimbaran and the luxury hotels spread along this coast, there is a clear view of jets lining up at Ngurai Rai Airport under the protection of the great mountain and spiritual centre of Bali, Gunung Agung.

started in their homeland of Mexico. They stayed for six months and wrote the classic book about Balinese culture, *The Island of Bali*, first published in 1937. Many other fine books were written in those early days by visiting writers. Their works are still charming to read and not far off the mark when describing life as it was then. Even though considerable changes have taken place since, there is so much that is the same.

Few foreigners visited Bali in the years following World War II and it was only in the 1970s when Australians and backpackers from distant places began to arrive in large numbers, having found Bali an inexpensive and exciting vacation destination. They stayed in basic *losman*-style (homestay) dwellings, the Balinese version of the bed and breakfast. Small cottages were built in the style of *bale meten* (sleeping pavilions) within the family compound to accommodate foreigners and to increase the family income. *Losman* rooms were very simple and clean, and the affordable daily rate included a delicious fruit salad

and banana crepe breakfast with dark roasted Bali coffee. Modern Bali *losman* are still popular as they make a charming and economical way to stay with the locals and learn about their lifestyle.

Balinese architect I. Gusti Nyoman Lempad's adapted *wantilan*-style dwelling for tourists set a trend that began with the house he designed for Walter Spies in the late 1920s. This style—of large, open-air pavilions often with two-tiered roofs—proliferated from the 1980s with rising demand for long-term housing. In particular, tourists wanted an individual house with a basic kitchen and a bathroom in a garden-like setting. As a result, many Balinese landowners near the tourist centres built either *wantilan*- or *lumbung*- (rice granary) style accommodations on their valuable rice fields, since the immediate cash gain for less back-breaking work than rice cultivation was just too enticing.

By the beginning of the 1990s, luxurious gathering places for tourists were being built all over Bali. By then, the international airport had expanded with non-stop flights from many faraway places, electricity was available in most villages and Bali was connected to the world through modern communication systems. Restaurants serving the finest of foods from a variety of cuisine were everywhere. Bali had all the amenities that tourists love and they came in droves to visit and to set up their dream homes.

Modern architectural design in Bali developed easily because of stable weather conditions, an abundance of exotic materials and unrestrictive zoning regulations. Furthermore, Balinese construction workers were willing, able and often skilled and creative enough to execute what was desired. The result was an abundant and exciting array of architectural styles, ranging from the extraordinarily refined to the cozy to some with a joyous 'live-life-to-the-fullest' attitude. While the traditional architecture of Bali is uniquely and exquisitely Balinese, now there was a vast amount of new architecture for *tamu* that was infinitely impressive in design and quality yet still of an undeniable Bali style. The gathering places for *tamu* on Bali are without a doubt among the world's most creative architectural designs. This section showcases a small selection of private homes, resorts and restaurants.

Lumbung-style dwellings There is a *lumbung* or rice granary in almost every Balinese compound. Designed to store rice up high off the ground, it has a steeply sloping roof with rounded ridges to drain off rainwater. Beneath the enclosed rice storage area is an open platform where people can gather to chat when it rained.

The *lumbung* dwelling that has been adapted for tourists has a gabled roof and two floors. On the lower floor are an open verandah, a bathroom and a room for sleeping. Providing access to the second floor bedroom is a small stairway. The main structure is made of either bamboo or the local *kamper* wood, has an *alang-alang* roof and *bedeg* (woven bamboo) ceilings and walls. Windows are protected by bamboo bars while shutters ensure privacy when closed. Bamboo blinds shelter the open verandah from rain.

The bathroom consists of the toilet and a *mandi*, a tiled square receptacle that holds less than one cubic metre of water. A plastic or coconut ladle is used to scoop water for pouring over oneself while standing in the middle of the tiled floor. Water flows out through a small drain outlet in the floor. Pouring ladles of water from the *mandi* into the toilet is equivalent to a flush. In many *losman* accommodations and Balinese homes, the *mandi* is still the favoured means for bathing—it is refreshing to ladle quantities of room temperature water over oneself on a hot tropical afternoon.

Attached to the back of this little bamboo home is a kitchen. It comes equipped with a propane two-burner stove and if one were lucky, there might be a sink with cold running water. As the tourist industry boomed in the late 1980s, rice fields in Penestanan became littered with these simple, thatched-roof houses for tourists seeking an authentic Balinese experience.

A *lumbung* in a family compound. The design of rice granaries such as this has been adapted to accommodate guests.

ABOVE Dutch colonial-style entry, as might have been built in Yogyakarta in the 1920s, leads into the Walter Spies pavilion at Hotel Tugu Bali. The blue-painted iron gate is from his home in Yogyakarta.

OPPOSITE Side view of the Walter Spies house at Hotel Tjampuhan shows details of the double-tiered *alang-alang* roof. The opening in the gable end of the second-storey roof allows air to flow through.

The Houses of Walter Spies

A dark brown two-storey house clung to the side of a steep ravine. Dense foliage screened it from the road and made a secret stillness. Below the house, an oval swimming pool lay half hidden among the trees, fed by bamboo pipe from a hillside spring. The house was decorated with Balinese paintings and antique carvings. One of Mr. Spies' own paintings, a forest scene in great detail with great shafts of light casting long shadows, hung in the living room. There was a grand piano as well—a remarkable thing to find in such a place.

Mr. Spies, tall and dignified, about forty years old, received us cordially and we were soon joined by Miss Vicki Baum, her brother and another German. Miss Baum was doing research for her novel A Tale of Bali. Two handsome young Balinese men served us whisky and soda.

At the swimming pool later, Mr. Spies introduced us to another handsome young Balinese, invited him to show us how well he could swim and dive and watched him with proud solicitude. The servants brought a low table laden with bottles, glasses and ice and set it in the water at the shallow end of the pool. Mr. Spies, lying partly immersed, poured the drinks. I sat up to my waist in the cool mountain water, holding a glass of Holland gin and imagining what exotic parties could take place in that hidden ravine. At night, the wooded slope would be mysteriously lit by burning wicks set in hanging coconut shells. Metal threads in the servant's garments would shimmer in the warm glow. The air would be a little heavy with burning incense and with the odour of coconut oil in freshly washed and anointed hair. That was an impression to take away.

— Louise G. Koke. Excerpt from her book Our Hotel In Bali, about her visit with Walter Spies in 1936 for advice on how to go about building in Bali.

Walter Spies—composer, musician, painter, writer and perhaps even a renaissance man (as many have named him). His life and times in Bali, although only a short 14 years, are of legendary proportions. He left an imprint on all of the arts of Bali including dance, drama and gamelan music. His homes were gathering places for celebrities, the well-to-do social set and researchers from every field of study from around the world. He was a charming host, knowledgeable tour guide and the person to ask about the real culture of Bali for no other *tamu* knew more of the people and the island than him.

Spies was born on 14 September 1895 in Moscow where his father was a German diplomat. The Spies family had actually lived in Russia for generations but they were classified as Germans during World War I and were thus detained in the Urals. As a young man growing up in post-World War I, he was in close contact with many European avant-garde artists and film directors. Spies apparently felt a need "to free himself of indoctrination and prejudices about taste and beauty and to freely paint as a child with the skill of Chagall and Klee," as he wrote in a letter to his father. In searching for himself, he travelled to Java in 1923 where he stayed with the royal family of Yogyakarta in their palace. He was then invited to visit Bali by the royal family of Ubud. So taken by what he saw in Bali, he decided to make his home there. The king of Ubud gave him a plot of land to build a home on a river ravine in the village of Campuhan.

I. Gusti Nyoman Lempad set about designing a home for Spies, in Campuhan, using the architecture of the traditional *wantilan* as a model. His adaptation of the *wantilan* design was revolutionary for it became a closed pavilion with rooms on the first and second floor. There was an open-air verandah, a bathroom and an enclosed space for sleeping or lounging on the first floor; the second floor was a large bedroom. A two-tiered *alang-alang* roof spread over the entire structure; the tiers surround the lower and upper floors but the roof just above the verandah was left open to the sky. Each tier had deep overhangs that offered protection from rain. Balinese traditional roof designs are truly exquisite in detail both inside and outside, the roof being one of the architectural elements defining Balinese architecture. Lempad's adaptation was so sensitive to proportion and details that it has since become a standard others have strived to match in both commercial and residential buildings.

Walter Spies led a busy life in Bali. He painted, studied gamelan music in all of its forms, composed music and re-choreographed old Balinese dances that had fallen out of use as well as co-authored a book with Beryl de Zoete. Their book, *Dance & Drama in Bali*, is still considered the best on the subject. He also intellectualized about the culture of Bali with notables such as Margaret Mead and Geoffrey Bateson while they made their anthropological studies and analyses, culminating in their well-known work *Balinese Character: A Photographic Analysis*. There was tension between Spies and Mead; he thought her method too scientific, cold and analytical, since he and de Zoete preferred a more aesthetic approach. Mead wrote of a meeting at Spies' home: "Walter fair and full of grace looked up from his conversation with Beryl de Zoete, with whom he was working on a book on Balinese drama and said, 'We'd given you up!'"

Spies' paintings of Bali landscapes included images of the *niskala and sekala* (intangible and tangible) world of the Balinese. His canvases had a surreal, almost dream-like quality with a dark, mystical ambience. He also painted the rural life of Bali and of ordinary people going about their daily lives. These everyday scenes, when depicted in works of art and when combined with the realization that such works could be sold, gave Balinese artists a different way of thinking about their art; until this time, they painted and sculpted without thinking about the concept of art-for-sale. Before the arrival of Westerners, Balinese fine art and sculpture revolved around religious subjects or characters from the Hindu epics, the *Mahabharata* and *Ramayana*.

Spies' home in Campuhan became the stopover for tourists looking for an exotic experience in paradise, since cruise

Living room of the Walter Spies pavilion at Hotel Tugu Bali. The stained glass is from his home in Yogyakarta. Other personal effects on loan from private collectors include letters, family portraits, an early camera used by Spies when he lived at the palace as well as his gamelan orchestra instruments.

ships—as well as millionaires' yachts—were now berthing in Bali. Ubud had become known as the place to visit on Bali. In an attempt to find peace and quiet, Spies built a second home in the mountains in the village of Iseh in the Karangasam district. This was also where he retreated to when he had to rent the Campuhan home to help with his finances.

However Spies' life ended in tragedy. He was persecuted by the Dutch in the pre-World War II years for his homosexual lifestyle and for holding a German passport, he was deported to Java with others in 1942. The Japanese then invaded Indonesia and Spies was put on a boat with other detainees to be transferred to another island. But their ship was bombed en route. The captain refused to unlock the cells and all prisoners lost their lives. This tragic death brought an end to the art and artistry of Walter Spies.

Today, his house in Iseh is privately owned. His house in Campuhan is available to rent at Hotel Tjampuhan. From his house in Yogyakarta, some furnishings and architectural elements are now part of the Walter Spies suite at the Hotel Tugu Bali in Canggu village.

Furniture and furnishings in the Walter Spies suite in Hotel Tugu Bali. These were originally in Spies' 1920s home in Yogyakarta. All were collected over a period of time by the hotel's owner, Bapak Anhar, from many locations and brought together to complete the suite.

ABOVE This bedroom in the Walter Spies pavilion at Hotel Tugu Bali contains furniture collected from his Yogyakarta home. The headboard was once an exterior gate from that home.

LEFT Part of the guest room pavilion at Spies' home in Iseh. From the balcony, one gets an amazing view of Gunung Agung and the valley floor of rice fields.

FAR LEFT This carved wood door to the Walter Spies house at Hotel Tjampuhan leads to an interior room that once held his baby grand piano. To have had a piano in 1930s Bali was part of the romantic ideals of the artist's life.

OPPOSITE This pavilion at Spies' home in Iseh served as his bedroom and studio.

Subak waters weave through the property of Talidandan, separating lawn from the rice field. The guest wing is just beyond the main pavilion, accessed by walking along the canal. Infinity edge pool follows the contours of the *sawah* and actually appears to be part of a field waiting to be planted. A perfectly proportioned four-post *bale* provides shelter from the sun and a peaceful place to lounge. The pool and *bale* are positioned on the edge of the river ravine; the dense forest of jungle provides privacy.

Talidandan — Walking Together with Sacred Threads

Talidandan, not far from Ubud, is a beautiful villa reached by way of a small, curving road that continuously ascends towards Gunung Batur. The views to either side of this winding track are of rice terraces so perfectly sculpted, you feel you are looking at a panorama painted with perfect perspective and designed with absolute balance and matchless beauty. Turning off this exquisite road near the village of Tegalalang onto a small road heading down to a river ravine, there sits a house of impeccable refinement.

Talidandan is comfortably settled into the rice field landscape; only the *alang-alang* grass roof is visible above the green *padi* (rice) from the approach road. The placement of the house is a successful blending of a man-made architecture perfectly threaded into the surrounding natural architecture of rice terraces and dense foliage of a ravine. Architect Joost van Grieken and owner Christina Welty were mindful of the pristine rural character of the area and carefully sited the house with sensitivity.

Christina has lived in nine countries during her life of exploring and working with different cultures; the past 20 years were spent in Japan. She explains with clarity of purpose how she envisioned her home:

"I grew up in a family of six in a small country town in California but at the age of 20 began to move and explore and develop, and for each inward step that I seemed to take, I moved. So it was with some anxiety that I decided to build, to put myself down somewhere and stay. After encouragement from friends, I finally planned a trip to Bali. I had lived in Asia for 25 years and had never travelled to Bali, fearing that the 'romantic place' would be an un-revolutionary diversion or a sad experience. I discovered Bali is rural with a deep culture and I could again become a student and drink deeply from the profound. Twenty months after my first visit I found the site that looked ordinary from the road but was breathtaking. It was a comforting site, like a natural cul-de-sac. One side with a long view of rice fields carried my imagination away, far away. Jungle provided one boundary while a hill provided the other.

It felt cozy and healing…I decided immediately. I interviewed many architects and builders but settled with Joost. His style was simple; he could deeply understand minimalism and blend Japanese elements with Balinese ones, and he lives in Ubud. I returned to Japan and began to plan a move after a 20-year stay. Joost and I met weekly, he listened, we talked and talked and gradually the house took shape. I wanted a house of profound space. I wanted a house that created experiences of awe. That meant art niches and empty walls and uncluttered spaces. While wanting a simple house, I didn't want a cold one. For me that meant wood and plants and textiles and carpets—'warm minimalism' was my motif. Ceremonies were held to ask the rice gods for permission to convert the land. Work was started and the construction site became home to 45 men, dogs, chickens, workers' hut, dust, mud, holes and bricks… it was difficult for me to imagine my home."

Now, two years later, Christina says: "Every time I enter the lobby I am still amazed by the overwhelming beauty at every turn, in every room. Awestruck in my own home! This is mine? 'More than yours', I keep thinking. I'm just passing through; this grandness must be shared, must be experienced by many. After all, this was the reason for its creation: to point beyond itself to something grand and healing and supporting to all who pass through. Even now I change the art monthly so there is freshness in our experience. In addition, art must be framed and surrounded by appropriate space to be experienced. Good art, whether it be an oil painting or sculpture or textile or flower arrangement, must grab the viewer's attention long enough to link with their life experience and call forth an emotional reaction, a familiarity. In that moment, the here and now is transcended by the broader, deeper mysteries and showered with meaning. So I named the villa *Talidandan*, which in Bahasa Indonesia means 'walking together with sacred threads', to proclaim the profound function of this space, to give deep refreshment to all who enter."

Talidandan successfully expresses the joy of a gathering place. There are remarkable spaces where friends and family can come together to enjoy tasteful architectural design so completely comfortable with the magnificent design of nature.

ABOVE The entry foyer sets a stage for a Zen-like peacefulness that can be felt throughout Talidandan. The freestanding art wall, like the traditional *aling-aling* found in Balinese compounds and temples, establishes a focal point and presents that 'moment' to leave the world behind and focus on the 'here and now'. The triangular art piece on the wall is by Australian artist Peter Dittmar. Within the niche is an old Archipelago bench and a wall to display artworks; currently hanging is a Kuba textile from Zaire. Flooring is a 'dry' polished sandstone (Javanese *wonosari* stones), bordered by black *batu yogyakarta*.

OPPOSITE Looking from the dining table towards the entryway is a view of the main sitting area. This raised area is enclosed and protected, yet open to the view because of encapsulating walls on each side of the banquette seating. The semicircular opening in the wall is not another niche for art but one that showcases Ramlan as he prepares yet another delicious lunch in the kitchen.

FOLLOWING PAGES Turning to the right from the main entrance, one steps across a fish and lily pond to get to the dining room. Lemon grass, a favoured seasoning in Balinese cuisine, is used as an attractive planting off the dining room. Across the lawn are views to the *sawah*. Note the column base, the *sendi* (bollard), which is a traditional feature of Balinese *bale* architecture. Here they are carved from volcanic tuff. Posts are polished coconut poles. Light fixtures are custom designed by the architect.

ABOVE The soaring *alang-alang* ceiling adds dimension and texture to the space above the free-standing wall that separates the main lounge area from a small sitting area beyond. The wall where the Japanese kimono is displayed is a *tokonoma*, a recessed wall for art. A Japanese tradition, *tokonoma* must have a raised floor and at least one side must be made of wood. Considered sacred for the exhibit of treasures, such niches are intended to focus one's attention on art, scrolls or flower displays. The midnight blue and purple silk kimono jacket with a butterfly motif is from Japan. Lacquered *tansu* chest is from northern Japan.

RIGHT Another *tokonoma* on the reverse side of the wall in the main seating area. This single wall conveniently divides the area as well as creates an additional art niche. The rare cotton *cepuk* sacred textile from Bali is one of the owner's favourite from her extensive collection. The artworks in the niches are changed often to enhance the experience of 'seeing anew'. The window in the guest wing has *washi*-paper vanes and looks into a garden separating the two pavilions.

ABOVE Christina's bedroom on the second floor is a private retreat, a suite of rooms separated from the rest of the house. Her balcony is perfect for an early breakfast and viewing the sunrise over the *sawah*. *Tansu* chest is from Japan. Sliding doors were made in Bali with proportions suggesting Japanese shoji designs. The resin-based *washi* paper used on the door panes is stronger than the traditional delicate rice paper. Floors are polished terrazzo. Rafters, door and window jambs and crossbeams are all *bengkerai* wood. Headboard furniture was designed by the owner and made in Bali.

LEFT The guest bedroom and private bath are examples of peaceful perfection. Batik design of the bed linen was custom dyed in Bali. The textile hanging above the beds is from Indonesia. The closet doors are made in the *yoshizu*-style, which in Japan are considered summer doors as the open-worked twigs allow for ventilation. Humidity is an important design consideration in tropical Bali. The guest rooms and the office are the only rooms with air-conditioning. The house design invites natural breezes and because it is at a higher elevation, night-time temperatures are pleasant.

A Stylish Cottage In Tebasaya

The narrow street passing through the village of Tebasaya in Peliatan is lined with compound walls interrupted by the entry gates of individual family compounds. A few of the walls have a recess large enough to set up a *warung*, a small family food business. Late afternoons, the *warungs* become busy as folks ending their workday have time to sit for a cup of Bali *kopi* and chat. Along the street, there is a *pura dalem puri* that is used by Ubud royalty for cremation ceremonies. And then there is the new Jazz Café, where local groups gather every night to play a mix of tropical jazz, traditional music and a little Balinese rap. The music must stop at 10:30 each night, an agreement reached between the owner and the *banjar* of Peliatan. It is quiet in Tebasaya although it is only a few minutes' walk from the centre of Ubud.

Halfway down the street on the right is a Balinese family compound with a small open-air café set into its wall. Walk beside this café towards the back of the compound and take the beautifully landscaped footpath that steps down towards the river ravine. Towards the end of the path sits a bungalow nestled in the contours of the land, surrounded by an exceptional garden that overlooks the lush jungle ravine. It is no surprise that the cottage and its garden are so exquisitely designed since the occupant of this Balinese bungalow with an oh-so-worldly interior is none other than Bill Dalton, landscape architect for one of the world's finest hotel groups.

This compact but functional verandah is attractively decorated with a hint of Indochine style. The cottage is a typical Balinese bungalow built for tourists in the late 20th century, with brick walls, *bedeg* (woven bamboo matting) ceiling and *alang-alang* roof. The teak steamer chairs, plantation chair and woven rattan chairs with ottoman are all from Bali. The slatted kitchen storage cupboard in front of the window is the upper part of a large 18th-century Chinese cabinet; its lower portion is in the dining room. Old and rare Burmese lacquered storage containers make a warm focal point when entering the porch. The stone-carved Buddha image in the foreground is *palimanan* stone from Yogyakarta, Java. The family temple stands in the garden to the left of the porch, wearing not the usual yellow or *poleng* sarong but a handsome blue batik fabric from Java.

Bill is always off to some distant place to design landscaping for a new hotel, to check the grounds for maintenance issues or to redesign a garden. His work has brought him to India, Thailand, Myanmar, Sri Lanka, Bhutan, Malaysia and about 20 other locations in very exotic places. Bali, however, is Bill's home base to which he happily returns whenever his very full schedule allows. Bill is from Hilton Head, South Carolina (USA) and in his sweet-as-honey voice drawls, "This house on Bali is a shoebox of a house but it suits my needs just perfectly." He plays with the idea of renovating to make a larger bedroom suite: "…just slightly larger," he says, "but in the meantime, it's just fine as it is." From a world that often associates larger with better, Bill Dalton's home is more than 'just fine'; it is 'near absolute perfection'.

The cottage is a useful study on how a small, well-designed home can have integrated spaces that play against each other in a functional and stylish manner, whether it is for entertaining a group for cocktails on the verandah or recouping in a cozy space after a long and tiring intercontinental trip. Bill's home is a comforting retreat from his busy life, a place filled with objects he has collected from around the world.

A comfortable rattan sofa nestles in the living room area surrounded by art collections. The large painting is not of a Balinese village but that of the compound walls and entry gates of the Amandari Hotel in Sayan near Ubud. Antique ivory figures were collected from around the world. The gold-leaf box is a Bible box that Bill found in Myanmar; it was found together with the original Bible, which has been dated to 1893.

OPPOSITE An impressive collection of rare 18th-century Japanese celadon porcelain is arranged on a stem-wall separating the master bedroom from the dining area. A beautifully carved Chinese teak table displays a polychromed wood carving of a *palebon baden* (royal cremation tower) being carried by villagers to the cemetery.

TOP LEFT A collection of silver containers and boxes on a teak chest of drawers in the master bathroom. They were collected by Bill on his many trips to Cambodia and Myanmar. Wainscoting is made of concrete tiles.

BOTTOM LEFT An old spinning device, an original Thai-silk spinning wheel, sits on a teak bedroom trunk from Java. Indonesian-born New Zealander John van Dersterran painted the landscape near his home close to Yogyakarta, Java.

ABOVE Balinese artist Made Kunatagoro interprets a rambutan tree and its fruit. The painting has a decidedly old-world character. Carved teak frame is by the same artist. Standard red brick walls painted white make a handsome textural background for this fine painting.

LEFT Although small, the totally functional kitchen has a smart, rustic feel. Bamboo *bedeg* cabinets under a stained-concrete tile counter top and backsplash repeat the organic feel of the bamboo and *alang-alang* ceiling. At the top right corner is an example of how bamboo is used for keeping out animals while allowing cross-ventilation, a detail often seen in Balinese architecture. Oriental patterned area rug is an antique Tabriz from Iran. Family pictures are a reminder of home at Hilton Head; the dark-haired beauty is Bill's sister.

RIGHT This extraordinary teak bed was custom made in Bali using traditional carving motifs often seen in the *canggahwang* (angled bracket) timber bracket designs on post-braces in pavilion architecture. The entire bed design is an adaptation of a *piasan* (a small, open pavilion for offerings) found in temple architecture. This large dynamic bed is an imposing choice in a small bungalow; however it is one that lends an air of importance and grandeur to an otherwise less than important corner of the room. Teak bench is from nearby Sayan. Painting was bought at auction during the estate sale of Emily Merriweather Post's Palm Beach home in Florida (USA). Glass in the gable end of the roof allows light to enter the cottage and adds visual interest and dimension.

Sheila on Seven

Every day here is a festival of visual and performing arts. What a joy to be living a life so full of new discoveries on a daily basis and to be constantly surrounded by creative, loving, happy people! I love sharing all this with friends and family when they come to visit. — Sheila Haisfield

Off the main road that leads into the village of Penestanan—actually Penestanan *kleod* (south Penestanan) near Ubud—is a small *jalan kaki*, a footpath meandering beside a brook-like stream of water, the *subak* irrigation waters. *Jalan kaki* are so narrow people must walk in single file, one-by-one like a line of ducks. Sometimes, a motorbike needs to pass and you must press yourself tightly against a compound wall to let it go by. Occasionally, a small bamboo or concrete gangplank is placed as a bridge to cross the *subak* waterway to a compound on the other side. Walking this path each day is a social occasion—meeting neighbours and learning what is new in the neighbourhood; greetings are always the question *"Mau kemana?"* in Bahasa Indonesia or *"Ke jao?"* in Bahasa Bali, both of which literally mean, "Where do you go?"

You will know Sheila Haisfields's house when you see the brilliant fuchsia bougainvillea hanging abundantly over the entry gate marked '7'. Sheila moved to Bali a few years ago, giving up her executive banking position in Palm Beach, Florida (USA), to live permanently in Bali. When she first arrived, the Balinese could not quite hear the sounds of her name until one day, someone said, "Oh, like Sheila on Seven!" which incidentally was the name of an Indonesian rock band and from then on she has been 'Sheila-on-Seven'.

Sheila leased a rather ordinary house and immediately began renovations to achieve a stylish and comfortable home. Her neighbours began to call her *ibu bankar* ('ibu' being the polite form for mother or Ms, and 'bankar' which means 'knock down') as she knocked down one wall after another. On Bali, foreigners may not own property and must have a Balinese partner if they want to purchase real estate. Since it is affordable to renovate, the more common approach is to lease property for the long-term.

Once through the entry gate there is an immediate view of this elegant three-storey house positioned to one side but completely embraced by an abundantly planted tropical garden. Sheila and her gardener, I. Ketut Sumarma, have transformed the entire plot, surrounded by high walls, into a garden filled with delightful vignettes of seating surrounded by flowering orchids and water gardens. To the right of the entry gate is a small *gudang*, or storage area, for shipping and receiving the hand-painted women's resort wear that Sheila and a partner design and develop for their business, Wild Ginger.

Steps leading up to the decks and verandah bid an inviting welcome to enter this cheerful house. An outdoor dining porch overlooking the family temple and lotus pond is the perfect breakfast spot to watch birds and butterflies or to see which orchids have opened.

On the first floor of the house is a living room, a dining area with kitchen to one side and a guest bedroom with a large garden bathroom. The second floor is Sheila's office and sitting room; both rooms are completely open to nature and only a blowy rainstorm requires the bamboo blinds to be lowered. Glass sliding doors separate the office balcony and bedroom suite. The third floor, also an open-air pavilion, contains a comfortable massage table and some seating to relax after a fabulous Balinese-style massage. Here again, bamboo blinds give shelter from monsoon weather.

This house is comfortable for entertaining both a small dinner party and a large gathering like the birthday party Sheila had planned for her grandson's 14th birthday. The celebration featured a gamelan orchestra, *legong* dancers and a banquet of food that included the Balinese specialty, *babi guling* (roast suckling pig) and all of the traditional accompanying dishes. Sheila has made a permanent home for herself here on Bali, only leaving the island for special visits with family or for business. She has made a richly textured and fulfilling life for herself in Bali.

Ever-blooming bougainvillea hangs luxuriantly over gate number '7'. Orchids and bird's nest ferns have voluntarily attached themselves to this river-rock wall.

The winding path is an enticing invitation, but then there is a bit of mystery as to just where it might be leading. Frangipani, various palms and a tall jackfruit tree shield a lofty three-storey façade, visually transforming the height to a comfortable scale. The office and bedroom suite on the second floor are practically concealed by the foliage. On the third-floor massage balcony, bamboo blinds have been lowered to give shade from the afternoon sun. Upturned roofs, an influence from China, are a popular feature in traditional Balinese architecture.

View from the teak deck across a few stepping stones over the lotus pond to the outdoor dining area and family temple. *Pembantu* (one who helps) Ibu Wayan Muklin places offerings each morning at the family temple located at the back wall. Teak steamer lounge chairs made in Bali are an invitation to gather in this quiet garden setting. Purple *umbel-umbel* are pennants used at temple ceremonies and other festive activities.

The living and dining rooms and kitchen are filled with light from the many windows and doors looking out to gardens, decks and dining areas. Decorative flower-like insets on the far wall are pierced for ventilation, as are the open bamboo transom above the windows. The furniture is locally made from hyacinth grass. The cantilevered console shelf, made of volcanic lava stone, is anchored through the wall and becomes a display shelf in the guest bedroom on the other side of the wall. The counter and bar tops are coloured concrete, polished to a smooth finish and waxed. Sandstone Buddha is from Singakerta, Bali. The flower arrangements were not made for this photo but are kept fresh daily by the hands of the very artistic Ibu Wayan Muklin. The flowers for these arrangements come from the garden. Musical instrument collection was gathered from around the Indonesian archipelago. Paintings are by young Penestanan artist Wayan Purnata.

T-houses — Minimal Impact Living

British architect Tony Gwilliam designed the T-house with a philosophy of environmental stewardship uppermost in his mind and heart. T-houses are modular so that any number of rooms may be configured to suit individual family needs. He thinks of such houses more like a well-executed piece of furniture or the fine workmanship of the components on a boat where each part not only has a purpose but is also aesthetically appropriate.

Tony designed the T-houses with a concept of forming a small community with simple housing, a plan for 'minimal impact living'. He has started such a complex in the village of Lodtunduh near Ubud on the edge of extensive rice terraces situated within a grove of bamboo, coconut, banana and jackfruit trees. There are nine individual T-houses positioned for maximum privacy, each with a view of the *sawah* landscape and spectacular Bali sunsets. Part of Tony's philosophy is to never build on the rice fields but to use land untillable for rice cultivation, which is usually on the edges of existing *sawah* or in river ravines. Many fruit trees, flower and organic vegetable gardens have been planted for communal sharing, as are the 14-metre lap pool, computer room and laundry room that are being planned.

Ironwood—which is extremely dense, impervious to termites and lasts indefinitely, even in the hot and humid tropical climate of Bali—is used exclusively in T-house construction. Cut and sawn in Kalimantan and assembled on site by village labour, the ironwood is oiled for the final finish; if left untreated, the wood develops a soft grey patina.

Gwilliam is the lead architect on the Lodtunduh T-house project along with architect Marita Vidal. The project's construction is by Nyoman Sarma and its project manager is Wayan Nama. For this project, the team agreed that the village of Lodtunduh was to be closely involved—neighbours helping neighbours—and so they taught the local people construction techniques and how to grow vegetables and plants the organic way. In keeping with the communal aspect of the project, the people are also being trained to offer maintenance, cooking and housekeeping services. Says Tony, "This is a win-win project. We learn local farming culture and crafts from the locals and we share our global knowledge with the villagers."

Before coming to Bali, Tony Gwilliam worked with Buckminster Fuller for many years and was actively engaged in the design and building of geodesic domes. This experience led Tony to the premise for the T-house: "The most efficient systems are the simplest. My basic philosophy has always been to build a house that improves the environment instead of compromising it. I want to help people reconnect to our past, each other, our planet, our universe—recreating a synergetic and co-creative relationship with nature, not a separation."

OPPOSITE Entryway to Tony Gwilliam's private T-house directs the eye straight through to the verdant *sawah* beyond. A small staircase leading to the bedroom above takes up minimum space and allows for maximum views. Exquisite sunsets from his verandah, just beyond the *kotatsu* table, encourage afternoon gatherings.

ABOVE Tucked into a tropical garden for shade and privacy, T-houses blend into the landscape rather than impose on it. This T-house has an *alang-alang* roof on the two-storey module and ironwood shingles on the meditation pavilion to its left. Sleeping rooms are located on both floors of the main structure and a semi-outdoor kitchen is to the right. A bathroom with outdoor shower shares a secret garden with the meditation *bale*.

LEFT Architectural skeleton of the second floor of a T-house under construction shows the mortise and tenon joinery. A *topi* (hat) is placed at the peak of the *alang-alang* roof; however, a closer inspection reveals that it is capped by an authentic piece of 'sculpture'—the neighbourhood black eagle canvassing the jungle.

The actual footprint of a T-house is small, but all rooms are organized for optimum use like the rooms on a boat. There is a feeling similar to traditional Japanese design. Beautifully proportioned sliding doors open to the breezes and integrate the indoor and outdoor spaces. Here, in this meditation pavilion, a *kotatsu* table for dining can be lowered into a recess if a larger floor area is desired. The bridge to the meditation pavilion is over the water garden that surrounds and flows under portions of the T-house.

Pantulan

Building this house was a magical experience. The site gave us cues to create an environment in harmony with the surroundings and we enjoyed the freedom to make decisions and changes as they were felt, not dominated by the rules and regulations so prevalent in many projects.

— *Architects Marita Vidal and Tony Gwilliam*

Reflection can mean 'meditation' or 'pondering' or even 'observation', and any of these are appropriate names for this contemplative house in the rural and quiet village of Lodtunduh. 'Pantulan' is on the signpost marking a narrow lane leading to its front gate. *Pantulan* means 'reflection' in Bahasa Indonesia; however, in this language, this single meaning relates to the reflection of images and how light plays at different angles, echoing visual impressions of its surroundings. Architects Marita Vidal and Tony Gwilliam designed Pantulan with strategically placed planes of water. They wanted to mirror the rice fields, the buildings and the magnificent starlit and moonlit skies of night or reflect the glorious clouds and sunsets of the day. The view from the entrance takes in two ponds—the first lined with dark green stones; the second, a lotus water garden—then the view continues to the swimming pool with an infinity edge and finally, to the mirror surface of the wet rice fields beyond.

Architect Vidal explains: "We wanted to work with the site, to work the pavilions into the landscape and treat the house as part of the village. Pavilions are a traditional Balinese concept but instead of closing the house off from the landscape, we opened it to the island. This required very careful placing of the buildings to preserve the trees and views. The main garden is the ever-changing rice fields; the house is orientated towards this magnificent vista. Other outdoor spaces are treated as special, intimate and magical corners belonging to their pavilions."

Vidal and Gwilliam had worked with owners Martin Reubin and Jacqueline Wales on building a previous home in the United States and were familiar with their preferences. They understood their need for social interaction with friends and family, and particularly their need for private spaces. Jacqueline is a writer and Marty needs a quiet space for meditation. They knew the couple's passion for good food and entertaining friends, so the living areas of the house needed to interact with the kitchen.

Since Jacqueline's interests include developing healthy, nutritious menus with exciting tastes, the kitchen not only had to be a joyful space to work, it had to be equipped with all the modern conveniences. Unlike traditional Balinese houses, this kitchen is integrated into the main pavilion but separated from the dining area by a custom glass-and-teak cabinet designed by Vidal and made by construction supervisor Wayan Nama. Glass doors permit light from the kitchen to reflect on the beautiful serving pieces stored in the cabinet. Interestingly, when standing at the end of the dining table looking towards the cabinet, the image of the Buddha figure that sits on top of the cabinet is reflected twice in the polished surface of the dining table. This is truly a sight to behold.

According to the architects, the plan of the house is based on three elements: a floor platform without interruption, wooden posts on a strict axis and a thatched roof over all pavilions. This floating-pavilion concept gives a feeling of being on a protected island surrounded by a sea of rice, each island connected to the next by a covered walkway. Another precept was to minimize energy use and eliminate the use of air conditioning. This required an open design with overhanging roofs to maximize the prevailing airflow while providing shade and shelter from rain. The only enclosed, air-conditioned room in the house is the audio/ visual media room.

The main entry to Pantulan has views across a reflecting pond to a lotus pond, the infinity edge swimming pool and then to the main water garden—the natural reflecting waters of the *sawah*.

Reflections are an ever-changing art at Pantulan.
This view is towards the dining room. On the left
is the main entry.

Long, connecting passageways with strong Balinese architectural elements, such as the *alang-alang* roof, structural posts and *batu paras* walls, give the house a strong, masculine energy that is softened by the use of warm *merbau* wood. This wood is used throughout the house as structural wood and for custom doors and window trim details. Terrazzo and stone are flooring materials for ground floors while *merbau* wood is used for the flooring in the bedrooms upstairs. Pantulan reflects traditional Balinese architecture in its open pavilion style and in the massive bamboo, wood and *alang-alang* roof.

Wayan Nama felt a positive atmosphere working on this project—everything seemed possible to him. The local construction team that he assembled was willing to experiment and try new ideas. The villagers of Lodtunduh contributed their traditional knowledge and learned new skills to create a beautiful, unadorned, hybrid Balinese-Western house.

Jacqueline recounted a charming, heart-warming story about the *batu paras* wall in the sitting pavilion. She and the architects held many discussions on how the wall would be treated since it was such an important focal point that led from one pavilion to the other: should they hang a painting, a wall textile on it...what? The homeowners and architects were away for a few days and upon their return, were surprised to see what the local villagers had done to it: they had carved a relief of a Balinese landscape on the wall. Beautifully conceived and executed, all agreed it was the perfect solution and a beautiful gift from the villagers.

Pantulan's open-air pavilions allow fluid movement from one area to the other and provide the perfect gathering places for friends and family. The clean lines of this Balinese architectural adaptation reflect the considerable taste and talent of the owners and architects, their understanding of traditional techniques and how they have applied these techniques successfully to a modern concept.

The dining and sitting pavilion look back to the front main entry and across the lotus pond to another sitting area. Artwork was collected throughout the Indonesian archipelago.

LEFT Sitting pavilion just off the master bathroom. The *batu paras* wall depicting a Balinese village scene was created by stone carvers of Lodtunduh village. The carving was a surprise gift for the owners when they returned from their trip away from Bali.

ABOVE Welcome to Pantulan! The entry courtyard has room for guest parking.

A massage *bale* anchors the sunbathing area of the swimming pool and provides a shaded poolside lounging area.

LEFT Organic thatched roof and polished *merbau* wood give the second-storey master bedroom a calm, sophisticated atmosphere. Sliding louvred windows control light and strong breezes. Built-in storage closets are strategically placed behind the bed. Furniture and fabrics are from Indonesia. Well-designed mosquito netting is from the workrooms of Wirata, a leading designer and maker of mosquito nets and owner of the Sama-Sama Shop in Campuhan.

ABOVE Large, sliding *merbau*-wood doors are louvred for ventilation but stand open most of the time to bring the outside indoors.

LEFT Young bamboo forms a handsome sculptural garden, a focal point for this outdoor guest bathroom. The rain bar is redundant in the monsoon season but a welcomed shower in the dry. Striate concrete walls have vertical textural interest, mirroring the thin bamboo stalks.

ABOVE This guest shower/bath area is near the pool and meditation *bale*. The shower enclosure and free-standing wash stand are a creative design solution, changing what can be a mundane cabana bath into a visually exciting garden bathroom.

LEFT Open clerestory of the kitchen creates a beautiful window to the rich foliage surrounding the site and enables good cross ventilation. Cabinets, counter tops and floors are terrazzo. Geometric vents in the wall allow for further ventilation.

ABOVE A small two-storey T-house next to the swimming pool offers a place for calm meditation downstairs and is a writing studio for Jacqueline upstairs. A lily pond flows beneath the *kotatsu* table.

A Tropical Oasis in Seminyak

I bought the land because of the trees, then trying to layout a house without losing one of them became a fantastic challenge. Finally, I pegged the shape of the house around the trees, connected the pegs with a red string and decided, this was it, this is the house. I really didn't draw a plan, just built the house to fit among and around the trees.

— *Michael Pritchard*

The site of Michael Pritchard's Legian home was completely covered with fabulous old trees and bushes. Cutting them down was not an issue for discussion and so the house was set to the back of a very long and narrow plot and designed between and around the largest trees.

Michael loves the high energy of the beach villages near Kuta and needed to live close to his businesses in Legian and Seminyak. He has had a home in the area for years, so when this jungle of a city lot became available, he knew immediately that he wanted to build a house for himself there. The site for this house was a long, narrow urban plot that was larger than needed for his personal house. Michael decided to build a guesthouse on the front half of the land, while his own home would be built on the back half. To save on building and maintenance costs, Michael designed a linear swimming pool that could be shared by both dwellings. The swimming pool is divided by a bridged wall to ensure privacy for both sides. The water flowing under this wall from one side of the pool to the other adds interest to the garden courtyard and pool area.

Water flows under the wall of this swimming pool that links the guesthouse in front to the owner's private house. The feel is that of a lush tropical jungle, a pleasant oasis in the midst of busy Kuta.

ABOVE This gathering room for parties is equipped with a built-in bar of unpolished black lava stone with front and back glass doors lit from the interior for an entrancing night-time impact. The glass wall behind the bar marks the stairway up from below. Furniture was custom made to proportions specified by Michael. The large painting is by Ngurah Atmaja from Selat. Floors are polished lava stone. Contemporary light cylinders are suspended from a mahogany plinth hung from the high ceiling.

OPPOSITE RIGHT Suspended balconies blend into the foliage of old, exotic trees. Glass sculpture is by Seiki Torige. Ironwood shingles make a maintenance-free choice for roofing in a densely shaded site.

OPPOSITE FAR RIGHT Doors on off-centre pivots allow positioning to catch the breeze or reduce airflow if it gets too windy. Such detail is used on windows and doors throughout the house. Glass is left clear in most locations.

Michael is the person to call on in Bali to design and orchestrate extraordinary events. He is known for creating fabulous oversized tropical flower arrangements set in unusual vessels, which he finds or makes from natural, organic materials; all this is done in his Legian shop called Heliconia. Michael also owns a gallery *Galeriesoklusa* in Seminyak, which specializes in glass sculpture and glassware from the studio of glass artist, Seiki Torige. It is in this gallery where Michael hosts an annual exhibition of these glassworks, an event not to be missed. The stunning displays of glass inventions are further enhanced by one dramatic exotic flower arrangement after another.

Michael's house speaks to his artistic nature. He has built a house that captures some traditional Balinese elements worked into a smartly contemporary home where he can gather his clients, friends and family in an ultra-modern setting. The house is awash with changing light: silhouettes of garden foliage play through textured glass walls on to walls of black, orange, squash yellow, red and sage green. Sea breezes set the garden foliage into a waving motion that brings the house alive. Night-time scenes have an even more dramatic effect achieved by garden lighting and recessed, hidden fixtures in each room.

TOP LEFT Polished Yogyakarta black lava stone on stairway reflects natural light filtered through textured glass wall panels. Recessed lighting recreates a similar feeling at night. Accent walls of pure pigment colours add drama to the black floors.

TOP RIGHT A high lava stone wall separates the galley kitchen from the dining area. Counter tops are ceramic but made to look like slate to complement the lava stone floors. Glass dinnerware is by Seiki Torige.

BOTTOM LEFT Sugar-palm seed in a vessel of *batu palimanan*. Lights suspended from the ceiling intensify this dramatic arrangement.

BOTTOM RIGHT A niche for built-in cabinet and art. The heliconia arrangement is in a container made from a chunk of glass from the workshops of Seiki Torige.

The glass endwall at the far end of the dining area, with vertical glass panels running from the floor to the ceiling, is visually interesting. The top half is open to the elements while clear glass fits snugly between the panels in the bottom half.

Puri Naga Toya

Well into the mountains north of Payangan is an area of fantastic beauty where small rural villages are scattered among volcano-shaped hills covered in lush forests. Although situated only a few kilometres from Ubud, there is a slight change in weather conditions with milder daytime temperatures and cooler nights. Such weather, when combined with rich volcanic soil and frequent rain showers, favours the growth of a huge variety of tropical fruit trees and plants. The variety seems endless and includes cacao, rambutan, jackfruit, sapodilla and *salak*; every small sapling entwined with vanilla vines. Then there is the heavenly jasmine scent of coffee plants in bloom. Driving in this central part of Bali is an up-and-down, round-and-round adventure as the roads climb steep hills and then descend to deep river ravines thick with a jungle growth of banana, coconut and bamboo. This area is called *Buahan* (literally translated as 'fruiting'), an area celebrated by painters and poets for centuries as a place of incredible natural beauty.

The Ayung, one of Bali's major rivers, has carved a course through these hills, creating sharp cliff-side escarpments. On such a site is a home, an Indochine-Bali masterpiece that creatively integrates traditional Balinese architectural proportions, orientation and materials with interpretations of other oriental styles. The main villa consists of three separate structures—a master bedroom suite, a kitchen and a two-

TOP LEFT Colourful antique entry gate from Singaraja, Bali, is an immediate indication of the Indochine-Bali style house waiting just inside these doors. Carvings on the gate include the Boma to discourage evil spirits, while two retainers kneel in greeting. Stepping up and over the threshold is a detail seen throughout China and Southeast Asia because it is believed that spirits of evil intention are unable to negotiate the step.

TOP RIGHT The combination of paint colours on this traditional Balinese carved door gives it an Indochine look. Triangular recesses are for the placement of daily offerings. This gate leads from the swimming pool to a private entrance of the master bath. Flagging stones are from Bali.

LEFT The main entry gate is unusual in that it is an open-air pavilion that includes a sitting area. The bench is from a nearby village and has a distinctive design. The carved wood wall panel above it is an antique from Madura. The lion sculpture is an old Balinese decorative foundation piece.

The exterior view of the main gate pavilion appears to be that of a traditional *bale meten* in its proportion and style. A four-post *bale* (left) makes up part of the entry path from the gate pavilion. Lily ponds and a lush garden surround this quiet and welcoming spot.

storey living pavilion. Each building however, is separate yet interrelated, like a finely composed work of art. Away from the main villa is a large *bale* for deer, a horse paddock and a small bamboo *bale meten* (sleeping pavilion). The enchanting *bale meten* was the only structure left on the site when the owners purchased the land. It has been renovated to serve as a guest bedroom.

The main entrance to the compound is through a small sitting area decorated with an unusual bamboo bench. The entry gate's antique double doors from Singaraja open into a courtyard garden where there are many places to rest and view the variety of groves, ponds and garden sculpture. A small Chinese pavilion is carefully positioned in the fishpond and water lily garden. Streams gush over stones, creating little waterfalls and delightful gurgling sounds, thereby enhancing the sensual experience in this oriental-inspired garden. Stone paths lead from one beautiful garden spot to the next, arriving finally at a natural spring-fed swimming pool tucked into the contours of the land.

As in traditional Balinese compounds, the kitchen is a separate building and one of three main buildings in the compound. The largest of the buildings is a two-storey traditional Balinese-style structure with some rural Chinese and Thai architectural influences. The roof is made of ironwood shingles from Kalimantan. Its lower walls are made of stone with large folding or sliding wood window-walls and doors. The third building is a magnificent master bedroom suite with high vaulted ceilings and a working fireplace that is put to frequent use on cool evenings. Antique wood and glass panel doors on the master bedroom building were found in China.

The art objects throughout the villa were collected in China and Southeast Asia, including Vietnam, Laos, Thailand, Myanmar, Malaysia and Indonesia. The designers and owners of this mountain home, Pamela and Royal Rowe, have travelled or lived in all of these faraway places. They are inveterate collectors, always on the lookout for interesting artwork for its beauty or for the way it intrigues the mind or those that are just simply fun. Their collections have finally come home to Puri Naga Toya.

Intrigued with the Indonesian archipelago as an undeveloped area of the world, the Rowes explored the nuances of

Indonesian culture through its vibrant local village markets, diverse landscapes, its history and cuisine. In Pamela's words, "We found a simple lifestyle, a new way of living that would enhance our lives. Eight years after we took up residence in Bali, Royal decided to build our dream house. We both enjoyed the pleasures of ancient inspirations melded with urbane sensibilities. We decided to build an oriental pleasure-building; an oriental pavilion to be designed and carefully situated within the landscape."

The Buahan area was an immediate choice for both Royal and Pamela from their first visit. Here they would have the room they needed for a compound of multiple buildings and the space required for Pamela's animals, which include two horses. "Our intention was to have a home with a light and insubstantial feel, more about personalized comfort and design than about a fancy address, cavernous rooms or look-but-don't-touch furnishings. Each room has its own individual beauty and agrees with people who care enormously about little things. Quality counts but not at the expense of a warm, human, seductive atmosphere. The rooms are intentionally inviting so that you can get to know them a little better."

Puri Naga Toya expresses in a rare and distinguished manner the significant character and tastes of its owners. The Rowes have succeeded in building, decorating and furnishing a home with memorable style and unaffected grace. The home and the property are a stimulating and a delightful experience in sensuous details and jeux d'esprit.

OPPOSITE View of the back of the living pavilion. The handsome, creative roof design addresses a complicated, octagonal structure.

TOP Once past the open *bale*, a stone pathway leads into this incredibly beautiful and inviting open entryway of the living area. The windows on the upper floor enclose an octagon-shaped guest bedroom.

BOTTOM This bamboo *bale meten* was the only structure on the property when the Rowes contracted the land. The old, carved Balinese door has been polychromed to add a charming hint of colour to the natural organic tones of this little *bale* in keeping with the feel of the new structures. The tarp on *alang-alang* roof is often seen in mountainous areas to shield the grass from frequent exposure to moisture, an effort to extend the life of a roof.

ABOVE The master bedroom building as seen from the dining room. Ironwood-shingled hip roof with overhangs, carved posts and decorative *sendi* are typical elements of traditional Balinese architecture. Decorative wooden paddles are antiques from Kalimantan. Just next to the paddles is an antique oil lantern from Java, once used to light the screen for *wayang kulit* (shadow puppet shows). Green jardinière is from Sulawesi.

RIGHT Ornate carved wood and glass doors from China open out to the master bedroom verandah. Patterned terrazzo floors add interest to a largely chinoiserie-style bedroom. Reflected in the glass is a glimpse of the expansive mountain view as well as of our driver and talented photo assistant, I. Komang Sudarsana.

LEFT Sumptuous, elegant, warm and stylish, the master bedroom has steep cathedral ceilings in traditional Balinese materials. Gable endwall is faux-finished with an interesting texture and has a charming mural. The fireplace is made from carved *palimanan* stone. The exquisite Chinese bed is teak and was made in Madura. The Straits Chinese desk, also an antique, was found in Sumatra. Black rattan chairs from Bali complete the chinoiserie-style look. Mirror over fireplace is a reproduction from Java. The table beside the chaise lounge is an antique Hepplewhite table in the form of a fern tree. Unique bamboo chair is from the local village.

NEXT PAGE The guest bedroom is a luxurious combination of furnishings from around the Indonesian archipelago. Trompe l'oeil dado wall murals painted by Balinese artists complete this splendid room. The soaring octagonal ceilings reveal the extraordinary workmanship and detail of the underside of the ironwood-shingled roof. Black Portuguese bed is a reproduction made in mahogany by Bali Chippendale. Bed coverings are from Holland and Portugal. Chinese altar table was found in Penang, Malaysia. Bronze Dong Son-style drum is used as a bedside table. Bamboo floor mats are from Sulawesi and Thailand. Carpet in front of white ikat-covered sofa is from Turkey. Black lacquerware is from Myanmar.

ABOVE The living room architecture displays three diverse elements in harmonious balance: a dynamic traditional Balinese ceiling juxtaposed with highly decorative trompe l'oeil tile floors and a compelling window-wall that looks out on to a powerful mountain landscape. Vintage furniture is mostly teak and represents styles ranging from primitive to Dutch colonial and Straits Chinese.

RIGHT Pamela Rowe with one of her two dachshunds in the entry hall to the living room. The building behind, just visible across the courtyard, is the kitchen and staff quarters. The large overhang shelters the entry from the morning sun and heavy rain. Painted floor-tile pattern is adjusted to a smaller scale than the pattern found in the living room. The room to the right is a sitting room for small gatherings and a room that Pamela calls her room; she loves to read there in the afternoons.

ABOVE The study is a combination of warm colours, hinting at an Indochine style. Pamela has an extensive collection of reference books, including a collection of antique 'Indies' period books that proved to be invaluable in the process of building Puri Naga Toya. Mahogany bookcases were custom built for storage of books and their collection of artefacts from Southeast Asia. Geometric border and wainscoting add to the interest of this room and the adjoining stereo/television room to the right. *Wayang kulit* puppet is from Java.

OPPOSITE TOP Natural water from a clear mountain spring fills the pool, which follows the contours of the land. The pool water is filtered but no chemicals are added. Granite cleft tile from Java has an aqua tone and brown iron-ore vein.

OPPOSITE BOTTOM LEFT Corridor from kitchen to staff quarters continues the polychrome appeal of the Indochine style.

OPPOSITE BOTTOM RIGHT These exquisite antique doors from China, beautifully framed by trompe l'oeil designs, lead into the guest bathroom and out to a private garden. The armoire on the left is a primitive cabinet from Madura. Pillows on the art deco chair are encased with fabric from Laos and Sumatra. The antique jacket on the right, a ceremonial waistcoat for a small boy, is from Sumatra.

Rumah Frank

Here is a home completely renovated from its beginnings as a *lumbung*-style house that was built in the early 1990s for tourists who visited Bali for a few weeks and wanted something more than a hotel experience. Frank Olcvary, an American living in Greece, came to Bali for what was meant to be a short visit with friends but decided Bali was the place for him. He took this house for a 'short' term; it has now been more than 11 years.

From the beginning Frank loved the convenient location of his *lumbung*-style house as it was within walking distance to almost everything in Ubud. As he began to immerse himself in the development of the Bali Hati programme (see Chapter 4), which he conceived, he stayed put and began to renovate the house. Today, there is little to indicate it was once a *lumbung*-style tourist accommodation.

Frank loves to entertain so a large dining area was a must. This room is the main addition to the original footprint. The tasteful renovation of his home has a light and airy feeling because of the large sliding glass doors, soft beige and grey polished marble floors, white- and yellow-veined quarried stone walls and white-washed *bedeg* ceilings. The monochromatic colour palette is a refreshing foil to the lush emerald green of Bali's foliage and bright colours.

He also wanted a pool so that he could invite the local kids for a swim and went about converting a fishpond into a pool. This 'pool' was only 76 centimetres deep and looked very much like a large bathtub. A good friend sponsored the construction of a real pool to be built in the yard and Frank set about designing it. A swim at *Pak* Frank's house became so popular that there was no other choice but to construct a public swimming pool just for the Balinese. This was the beginning of Rumah Hati, a large public pool for the local children to use and enjoy. Community outreach is Frank Olcvary's mode of operation, his life, and if the determined and passionate Frank Olcvary has an idea, one might consider it an already accomplished reality.

Rumah Frank is also known as the 'Court of Miracles'. In the years Frank has lived in this house, he feels his life has been blessed with so many miracles. The Bali Hati project is one of those magnificent miracles.

OPPOSITE The monochromatic colour scheme seen here is a fresh approach to tropical, colourful Bali. The ceiling of the dining room follows the form of the hip roof and has whitewashed rafters and *bedeg* ceiling.

ABOVE Two pavilions near the swimming pool, one is for lounging (left) and the other with floor cushions serves as a dining pavilion.

Villa Ramadewa

Londoner Anthony Harrison had visited Bali many times because he enjoyed the spirit of Bali's culture and always left with a memorable vacation experience. Each time he returned, he found the island more and more to his liking and the obvious next step was to think of building a home there. Anthony was attracted to the beachside resort of Legian because it offered the possibility of having many interesting activities to do as well as a restful atmosphere for doing nothing. Furthermore, it has a wide choice of fine restaurants within the Kuta-Legian-Seminyak villages and the airport is only minutes away.

Anthony needed a home to serve as a gathering place for friends and business acquaintances, to bring people together in a comfortable yet stylish retreat. He admired conventional

Balinese design but was also very much taken by the modern, creative approach to the new homes that were being built on the island. He decided he wanted a home that would incorporate and complement basic Balinese architectural principles but with a more avant-garde approach. After sorting through many projects and architects, Tony asked Ubud-based Dutch architect Joost van Grieken to visit him in his London home to see how he lived and to get a feel of the type of space he enjoyed. While in London, Joost and Tony began to develop a concept for a Bali home that would be a retreat from business, yet be a practical space to address Tony's international business requirements while on Bali.

Tony remembers those early planning discussions: "I wanted a quiet haven where I could relax and escape from business when I needed to, but also needed to be able to do business and run the company from the villa when necessary. Hence I wanted a study which made working a pleasure. It was also important to be close to the beach. The villa had to be open and airy with large spaces to entertain. Entertaining is a major part of my life and I wanted to create a tropical haven in which to do this. I decided to have a kitchen that could be used for large dinner parties, where on most occasions we all end up in the kitchen drinking wine while cooking. I wanted to furnish the villa with both modern and antique furnishings, hence the Phillipe Starck appliances mixed with the old colonial and Javanese pieces. The art is a collection of pieces from around the Indonesian archipelago."

Villa Ramadewa has successfully adapted traditional Balinese architectural elements to become a contemporary Bali home. It adopts the architecture of pavilions with sleeping rooms and a study connected by a long corridor to the large gathering pavilion for dining and relaxing. Staff rooms, laundry and storage rooms are inconspicuously located along the corridor. A fabulous kitchen anchors the corridor near the gathering pavilion. A traditional Javanese *joglo* (decorative centrepiece used in early houses on Java) shelters the whirlpool on the right end of the swimming pool and provides a shaded place for exercise or just lolling about.

OPPOSITE Corridor leading from the guest pavilion towards the kitchen wing. Pink coral stone garden at the end of the gallery makes a textural and colourful focal point. A bamboo spout fills an old stone water container and starts the flow of water to reflecting ponds and fountains. Polished coconut-tree columns are a traditional Balinese architectural element.

ABOVE This grand 12-post *wantilan* is completely open to the outdoors but is equipped with large custom sliding window-walls that can be shut when air conditioning is a must. The *alang-alang* roof floats above this gathering space, sheltering it from the bright Legian sun or a sudden downpour. Teak furniture is by architect Joost van Grieken. Honed *paras* stone floors are bordered by quarried volcanic tuff. Ironwood from Kalimantan is used for the decking around the pool area. The pavilion seen across the lawn comprises two guest bedrooms on the first floor; the entire second floor is taken up by the master suite (*left*) with an outdoor sitting space separating the office and study (*right*). The ironwood-shingled roof of the swimming pool *joglo* pavilion shields the view of the rooftop garden with a sunbathing area.

ABOVE Sculptural leaves of the beautiful breadfruit tree compete with the stone artwork from Sumba. This view from the outdoor sitting area of the master bedroom shows the traditional *alang-alang* roof on the gathering pavilion. Bamboo crosswork on the thatched roof is a traditional technique used to secure the grass during windstorms.

RIGHT The clean design of the furniture contrasts nicely with indigenous materials (teak and woven rattan) to lend warmth to this seating arrangement. Ancient water jars from Indonesia have been adapted as water fountains, giving a tranquil aural accompaniment to the visually pleasing golden bamboo garden. Here is a great example of a static wall that enables the interplay of spaces—"both static yet directional"*—like the walled compounds of Bali.

*from Complexity and Contradiction in Architecture by Robert Venturi.

TOP A very smart looking kitchen with friendly staff preparing lunch for our photo crew. Cabinets are custom made of teak wood, with a black resin/terrazzo counter top. The open pantry displaying serving pieces has a glass rather than wood back in order to admit light from the entry corridor on the other side of the wall into the kitchen. Circular skylights in the ceiling and the rectangular windows in the curved wall of the breakfast nook play light around the kitchen.

LEFT The rooftop sitting area, with a garden and private sunbathing spot, overlooks a view to the pool and sculptured lawn. The ironwood-shingled roof shelters the swimming pool pavilion. Tiled roof in the background belongs to a neighbour's house in the growing suburban area of Legian. A wall completely surrounds Villa Ramadewa like a Balinese compound, providing privacy and a secure, quiet atmosphere.

ABOVE The dining area of the gathering pavilion features art niches displaying old Balinese roof support columns. A magnificent custom-carved 2.5 metre glass door, designed by the architect and made in Baliu, opens to the art corridor. Off-centre pivot allows the door to swing in either direction.

LEFT Covered outdoor sitting area links the master bedroom to the study. Access stairway is around the back of the art display ledge. Louvred grillwork above seating deflects rain that gets past ample overhangs of the *alang-alang* roof. Having tall, polished *bengkerai*-wood posts standing outside the basic structure is an often-seen technique of traditional Balinese architecture. Floors are polished teak. Custom doors are *bengkerai* wood. Antique art objects were collected in Indonesia.

TOP The serenity of the master bedroom comes from the tailored, clean lines of the furnishings. Polished teak floors and *bengkerai*-wood doors were all made in Bali. The art corridor that connects the master bathroom with the private entry to an office is illuminated with a delightful play of light streaming in from narrow glass windows.

BOTTOM LEFT The dressing area of the master bathroom has shoji-like doors, which complement the airy translucent quality of the bathroom itself. Artwork and flowers decorate a niche above built-in drawers for clothing. Polished teak floors of the dressing room lead on to quarried volcanic tuff tiles in the wet bath area. A chiselled frosted glass window and skylight highlight a beautifully sculpted tub. Out of this view but to the right are the shower, water closet and double sinks.

BOTTOM RIGHT Toilets throughout the house are full of interesting architectural features, as in this guestroom toilet with a circular window that looks out to a coral-rock wall. The contemporary water closet is a Philippe Starck design.

RESORTS
Hotel Tjampuhan

Our holiday began when we arrived at the Hotel Tjampuhan in Ubud. Nestled into the slope above the Tjampuhan River, this cosy network of rustic grass-roofed bungalows with wide, cool verandahs was our first experience of a tropical paradise.

Each night, summoned by the call of the kulkul, *the traditional wooden gong with the male-like appendage, we gathered in the open-air restaurant overlooking a sprawling garden of brilliant flowers, flamboyant trees and ginger plants. The scent of coconut candles infused the air and provided a gentle light as we mingled with the guests. Balinese bamboo music drifted around us and tinkled down to the river. Mealtimes were like a temple procession of the senses. Young Balinese men and women wearing traditional shirts and patterned tea-coloured sarongs, each adorned with a single brilliant red hibiscus flower, brought exotic colourful platters of Indonesian food to each seated guest. I remember being spellbound by their beauty. Frogs' legs, spicy pink fried rice, green leaves tossed in peanut sauce, a variety of satay (barbequed meat on skewers), fruits poached in palm sugar and other unknown dishes were part of the foreign menu. It was the most aromatic food I had ever tasted.*

— Janet deNeefe's description of her first visit to Bali in 1974. She met her husband, Ketut, on a subsequent visit to Hotel Tjampuhan. She tells these stories in her autobiographical book Fragrant Rice: a Taste of Passion, Marriage and Food.

Hotel Tjampuhan* remains a place of romantic ideas and notions after more than 60 years of operation. It has always been a destination for those who have in mind a real experience of Bali. In the early days, it was the only hotel near the village of Ubud and quickly became the place where artists, anthropologists, biologists, archaeologists, writers and backpackers mingled with celebrities. The visits of famous people like Charlie Chaplin, Cole Porter, Noel Coward or socialite Barbara Hutton brought the hotel international attention. The location is ideal, being just one kilometre down Jalan Raya from Ubud heading towards the hamlet of Campuhan*. Here is a hotel with a real history.

Hotel Tjampuhan is owned by the royal family of Ubud. Its notable history began when German artist Walter Spies made his first trip to Bali and visited the King of Ubud, Tjokorde Gede Agung Sukawati. Today, the king's three sons, the three princes, continue to run the hotel and carry on its traditions. It is impossible to speak of the history of Hotel Tjampuhan without including Walter Spies. He loved Bali from the moment he arrived and the King offered him a site on a beautiful river ravine in Campuhan to build a house.

The house that Spies built sits at the convergence of two branches of the Wos River, the Lanang and the Wadon. The intersection of these rivers is believed to be a place of great magical and healing energy. According to an old *lontar*, the Hindu sage Rsi Markandeya was drawn to a place in central Bali with a great pulsing, white-light energy. This place was named Tjampuhan from the word *campur*, which means 'mixed' or 'combined'. On a beautiful site in Tjampuhan overlooking the Wos River, he built a temple—the Puri Gunung Lebah—which is still one of the most important temples in the area. Actually, all of Ubud was historically considered a place

LEFT Stone Boma carving above the entry gate to the grounds of Hotel Tjampuhan wards off evil spirits. Sentinels wrapped in *poleng* sarongs with the ubiquitous red hibiscus flower tucked behind their ears are two humorous characters—Twalen and his son Merdah—often seen in shadow puppet dramas. *Canang* offerings are placed here and throughout the hotel, gardens and rooms each morning.

*Hotel Tjampuhan and the village of Campuhan are pronounced the same. When a language was developed in 1949 for the new independent country of Indonesia, Dutch spellings were changed. Both the 'c' in Bahasa Indonesia and 'tj' are pronounced 'ch' as in 'change'. Hotel Tjampuhan was named at a time the old spelling was in use and remains part of its tradition.

of healing energy. The name Ubud is a derivation of *ubad*, or medicine, because of the large quantities of medicinal herbs that grew in the area.

After the untimely death of Walter Spies during World War II, the Palace turned his house and other bungalows that had been built on their property into guesthouses for tourists, calling the place Hotel Tjampuhan. Over the years, the princes continued to build and renovate the hotel and have included Walter Spies' house as a cottage available for tourists to stay. One of the princes, Prince Gede Oka Sukawati, is an architect and has personally designed many of the buildings on the property. Today, all three brothers are still involved in the operation of this hotel as well as their other properties in the Ubud area, the Hotel Pita Maha and the Royal Pita Maha. Each property is built in the traditional Balinese architectural style and has a true Balinese atmosphere.

Until 1976 Hotel Tjampuhan had no running water or electricity. One of the gardeners from that period, I. Ketut Karta, who is still a member of staff at the hotel, tells of the time when he had to carry large buckets of water on a bamboo shoulder pole up a steep ravine to every guest room. There he would pour the water into a *mandi*—a tiled or concrete open

receptacle—in the bathroom. To bathe, there was a coconut ladle to scoop water from the *mandi* and pour the water over oneself; the water would drain through an outlet in the tiled floor. Pouring a ladle of water from the *mandi* into the toilet accomplished the flush. At that time there was also no laundry; sheets, towels and guests' clothing were washed in the river and left to dry in the sun on rocks. People recall sheets hung out to dry on coconut fronds fluttering in the breeze.

In those days, the hotel had a small kitchen and dining room serving delicious Balinese and Indonesian food. In fact, the hotel was known as the place to 'eat out' in Ubud. If a guest wanted room service, he needed only to strike the wood or bamboo *kulkul* hanging on the verandah and a room boy would appear shortly. The *kulkul* of each room had its own distinctive sound and employees could easily recognize the pleasant hollow tones to know which room required service.

Breakfast, both Western and Eastern fare, was served on the verandah. A Western breakfast included banana crepes with honey, lime juice and a sprinkling of freshly grated coconut; eggs (as you like); and a slice of white 'styrofoam-like' imported bread (wheat is not grown on Bali and bread with a long shelf-life was imported to satisfy the palate of foreigners). An Eastern breakfast consisted of *bubur* (rice porridge) or spicy *nasi goreng*, which is fried rice cooked with large amounts of *cabe* (local red hot peppers) and a *sambal meta* sauce of fresh garlic, red shallots, torch ginger blossom, lime and *cabe*. Whether Eastern or Western, you absolutely could not go wrong except for the 'styrofoam' toast.

Although Hotel Tjampuhan has been modernized, it still retains its original, authentic atmosphere. The guest rooms, including Walter Spies' house, have been upgraded. The dining room has been enlarged and now overlooks the gardens and river ravine. The grounds of this hotel are outstanding with many steps and pathways leading past carved rock walls, stone and wood statuary as well as exquisitely designed gateways. Along the way, down the winding steps to the ravine, is the hotel spa, a grotto of hand-carved stones and rocks that looks somewhat surreal.

OPPOSITE Gardens and pathways at Hotel Tjampuhan wind past carved stone walls and statues tucked everywhere in this jungle, river-ravine setting. The hotel's spectacular gardens continue to win national garden competitions.

ABOVE Riverside *bale* for massage. Sound effects of rushing water and bird songs do not require stereo equipment in this natural setting. Batik covering is from Bali.

TOP LEFT The carved stone wall at the back of the restaurant at Hotel Tjampuhan leads to an art gallery for local artists. Supporting the art and artists of Bali has long been a tradition of Ubud's royal family. A tree grew where the new dining room was planned. Instead of being cut down, the trunk was carved and is now an organic sculpture in the middle of the dining room.

BOTTOM Morning light illuminates the verandah of the Walter Spies house at Hotel Tjampuhan. The opening in the ceiling over the dining table allows air to flow to the second-storey roof. Windows of the upstairs bedroom look down to the dining table below. Walter Spies had a baby grand piano in the first floor room. The verandah was and still is a place for gathering.

Taking the steps further down to the river, past thatched brick-and-stone guest cottages, the winding path intrigues and surprises at every turn. Sculptures are tucked everywhere amongst starfruit, mango and jackfruit trees, and ferns and ancient frangipani trees that perfume the night air. And then there are the birds that chatter and dart through the trees; there is one that is especially startling as it flashes along the ravine, always plying the river for food—the bright blue Java Kingfisher with its orange-red beak. Down by the river, there are also two old stone beds built by Walter Spies for his guests to sunbathe. Cross the footbridge over the river and up to the top of the ridge, you will reach Puri Gunung Lebah, the temple that Rsi Markandeya built and which plays an important part in the spiritual life of the people at Hotel Tjampuhan and the villages around Ubud.

For more than a half century, Hotel Tjampuhan has been the hotel of choice for those nostalgic for a Bali they once knew or for those searching for a true Balinese experience within the convenience of a hotel. Traces of the past remain in the architectural details of the buildings and gardens, and in the small details like the placing of red hibiscus flowers on every possible surface. A sense of history is also felt when meeting staff who are like old friends; they are part of the legacy of the very romantic Hotel Tjampuhan.

Hotel Tjampuhan's spa is a fantasy world of nymphs, monkeys, mystical animals, flora and fauna carved on every possible surface of this cave-like grotto on the edge of the river ravine. Whirlpool baths of different temperatures are all fed by natural springs from the Campuhan ridge. This view is of one room of several, all of which are entirely covered in these fantastical carvings hand-chiselled into stone and cement. The red hibiscus flower is a trademark of the hotel.

ABOVE Absolute, understated elegance is evident in the main pavilion of the Amandari. The view is from the bar lounge towards the front desk and main entry. Coconut-wood posts sit on white stone *sendi* (bollard). Floors are polished marble and rough quarried slate from Java. Furniture is teak from Java.

LEFT The living room area of the Villa Agung suite looks out to a private plunge pool. Architect Peter Muller has received awards for the classic villas of the Amandari Hotel. Lounging beds are reminiscent of *bale dangin* sleeping beds, which provide the post supports for such a large roof system. Following traditional *bale* architecture, the posts terminate on *sendi*. Sliding glass doors that open the entire first floor like an open-air pavilion but can be closed for air-conditioning were the inspiration of designer Carole Muller. All 'loose' furniture and fabrics at the Amandari were chosen by Australian interior designer Neville Marsh.

Amandari

If there is one hotel in Bali that stands out in a long list of fabulous upscale hotel properties, it is the Amandari in Kedawatan, near Ubud. The Amandari is indeed an outstanding example of a design that has succeeded in adapting traditional Balinese elements to achieve a newer, more refined atmosphere. Walking the garden paths to the individual villas at the Amandari is like strolling along a quiet street in a beautiful and tidy Balinese rural village.

Says architect Peter Muller who designed and supervised the construction of the Amandari in 1987: "The basic concept behind the design of this hotel was to emulate my remembrance of the typical Balinese village layout I saw in the 1970s. The streets were wall-lined in stone or compacted mud with gateways to each family compound. There was no street planting then; it was something introduced much later in the form of a government-sponsored program to 'beautify' the village landscape, a programme that completely destroyed the unique aesthetic of the Balinese village. The individual villa construction at the Amandari followed Balinese principles of placing the roof construction on top of a system of coconut and teak columns, the solid *paras* walls being added later as infills without structural purpose."

Muller had previously designed and built a group of residential villas in 1972 using the Balinese *bale*-style roof. His adaptation, however, was to place the roof on solid masonry walls instead of an array of coconut columns. The foundations were traditional Balinese without the use of reinforced concrete. These villas became the Oberoi Hotel in Seminyak in 1977, and Muller has been involved ever since in its upgrading and extensions. Peter Muller's designs at the Oberoi and the Amandari provided an engineering answer that resolved the issue of thickets of posts required to support large *wantilan* structures. Others have used his solution and have creatively adapted traditional Balinese architectural elements into modern structures, both commercial and residential.

Strong structural elements and warm wood panels anchor the main dining room at the Amandari in near perfect proportions. Dining tables line the outside perimeter of the *bale* under a covered balcony that overlooks the deep river ravine of the Ayung River. Teak panels surround a private interior dining room. A carved Boma sits on cross beams to keep out evil spirits.

The Amandari overlooks magnificent views of terraced rice fields cascading down to the Ayung River. Exotic gardens abound at every turn and corner and perfectly complement the compound walls that surround each villa. Pathways meander through the gardens lined by the walls, interrupted by gateways into the villas. The hotel, the grounds and the furnishings for the interiors, such as built-in casegoods, fixtures and lighting, were designed by Peter Muller.

Most architectural critics will agree that the award-winning Amandari remains the most authentically designed adaptation for luxury hotel accommodations among a huge field of newer entries. The Amandari's design is one of quiet elegance; it is pure in form and represents a simplicity that achieves a visual remembrance of a traditional Balinese village.

The Amandari's swimming pool duplicates the terraced rice fields that step down towards the ravine overlooking the Ayung River. The *bale* across the pool serves as a stage for the gamelan orchestra and Balinese dance performances.

Hotel Tugu Bali

There is a private, residential atmosphere that can be felt from the moment of arrival at the Hotel Tugu Bali; it is as if a friend has invited you to stay at their luxurious home filled with works of art and valuable antiques. This delightful place has a personal, intimate quality to the interior spaces and gardens.

Hotel Tugu Bali is a boutique hotel with a mission statement—to preserve the rich cultural heritage of Indonesia through the exhibition and conservation of artworks, antiques and objects that tell a story of the diverse history of this country. The vision of its owner, Bapak Anhar Setjadibrata, is to provide luxury accommodation for those in search of a nostalgic journey into the past: "For me, the Tugu Hotels and Villas are a link to the romantic moments of this country, the forgotten history, and offer an opportunity to live in the luxury and comfort of modern times."

Hotel Tugu Bali achieves this vision by placing Bapak Anhar's vast personal collection of fabulous historical artefacts into close, personal settings that guests can touch and use. These objects are immediately apparent and within reach from the moment one enters the great *bale agung* lobby. The historic objects, the furnishings and architecture are all completely stunning. The hotel has successfully merged the feeling of a museum with the comfort and informality of a grand private residence throughout all 26 private rooms, the gardens and other public areas.

Bapak Anhar came to Bali from Java in the 1970s. He was a young medical student taking time off to travel to faraway villages throughout Indonesia. During his travels, he had a pivotal dream "of a big house lit by many oil lamps and candles, a residence adorned with hundreds of old antiquities that would make romance stay always, safe from the cold efficiency of modern changes". While wandering on the beach

of Canggu in Bali, he met a priest making offerings using a *capu manik*, a stone vessel for storing holy water. Some years later, he saw this same vessel in an antique store in Java, immediately purchased it and decided to build a big house on the same beach at Canggu. He brought the treasure back to the island from where it came. This 16th-century sacred ceremonial bowl now sits in the lobby of Hotel Tugu Bali.

At the age of 25, Bapak Anhar became interested in Ming dynasty furniture and collected some pieces from the period. He then began collecting objects from all over Indonesia including Dutch colonial architectural elements, such as posts, beams, windows and roof supports. "In the early '70s I was struck by the fact that Indonesians were throwing their culture away; they didn't recognize its value. Old furniture, tools, photographs, silver, gold were being tossed away, being replaced by modern things." He bought entire buildings to reclaim a few valuable materials; this included an entire 300-year-old ancestral Chinese temple in the heart of Jakarta that was doomed for wrecking. This temple was deconstructed and rebuilt at Hotel Tugu Bali as the Palace of Harmony, the *bale sutra* dining room for private dinner parties.

Bapak Anhar and his wife Ibu Wedya Julianti made sketches of their design concepts, which master craftsmen referred to when building the hotel, and closely supervised the construction. Their goal was to build a hotel in the style of a grand historical home, a hotel that would be an antique storage hall. The parameters they defined required a creative, new approach to typical hotel planning.

Moving away from convention, the owners opted for a series of private dining rooms along the perimeter of the lobby instead of a single large dining room. Each private room is furnished with an antique dining table, dining chairs and a sideboard or buffet server, all from Indonesia. There are other areas for dining throughout the property—a table here and there, even in the gardens that come with every guest room—and all are always intimate, private settings. Then there is the *warung* (informal food stand) where you can catch a bite of traditional Javanese food.

LEFT Soaring *alang-alang* ceiling in the grand *wantilan*, the *bale agung* lobby. The giant woodcarving of a mythical Garuda bird is by Nyoman Ada. In front of the counter is the *trompong*, an instrument in the gamelan orchestra; it is more than 100 years old. Woodcarvings of the protecting image of Boma look down from each post.

The lounge area off the main lobby is an intimate space. Art deco chairs were found in Java. The screen with shadow puppets is a relic but not a rarity since shadow puppet dramas playing out the beloved *Mahabharata* stories are still part of the temple ceremonies in villages everywhere.

Private dining rooms are lined along one perimeter wall of the main lobby. Curtains may be drawn and doors closed for more privacy. Each room looks out to a tropical garden.

Each private dining room has a high *alang-alang* ceiling, which gives the room volume and interest. On the late 19th-century buffet are two instruments from the gamelan orchestra as well as a mythical man-bird said to be the vehicle for Shiva. Light fixture is from the Dutch colonial period in Java.

A unique and personalized service extends to the spa facilities; a therapist comes to the guest's room and brings the guest to the room where the treatment will be held—there is not the usual front-desk check-in procedure and never is there a feeling of a large spa facility. Ibu Wedya Julianti has a medical background and has had a life-long interest in Chinese medicine as well as traditional health and beauty concepts. She brings these passions to the design of the spa and the creation of its spa services. All spa products are individually formulated for each client using natural herbs, spices and oils.

Lucienne Anhar, daughter of the owners, is in charge of the development of the luxury group Tugu Hotels & Exotic Spas located in Bali and Java. When speaking of the design process of Hotel Tugu Bali, she explains: "At the Tugu, there is a thin line between the physical design and the design of services. It is difficult to explain…a quality more easily experienced to be fully understood. For example, the *bale sutra* Chinese temple dining hall is beautiful but not complete without the complex Straits Chinese dining ritual that includes Qing dynasty plates and the Chinese Peranakan silver. Also, the *bale puputan* has

all the memorabilia but is not complete without the traditional Javanese/Dutch Rijsttafel dining ritual with twelve-waiters parade. My father's and mother's passions in designing the hotel completes each other; my mother brings the feminine touch to Hotel Tugu, as seen in the fabrics or flowers, and she creates and recreates all of the spa aspects of the hotel."

Traditional Balinese architecture is the overriding theme in the architecture of the hotel, with *alang-alang* roof structures on all buildings. However, each of the 26 guest rooms is decorated in a different style and period relating to the Indonesian archipelago. Two large guest suites were built and furnished with important authentic furnishings and archival quality artwork in honour of two artists of historic importance from the 1930s period in Bali: Belgian artist Adrien Jean LeMayeur de Merpres and German-born Walter Spies.

Although the entire process of designing and building the hotel took about two years, acquiring the treasures began more than 30 years ago and has not stopped. Hotel Tugu Bali is itself a treasure, a living museum where one can experience Indonesian life as it was but probably in never so comfortable or beautiful a setting.

LEFT *Bale sutra*, the Palace of Harmony pavilion, was once an 18th-century Chinese Kang Xi Buddhist temple. Today, it is a powerful reminder of Chinese-Indonesian cross-cultural ties. The hall is a private dining room in which a dinner fit for an emperor can be arranged: 'swallow is nesting' soup, crowned abalone, whole sharks' fin in oyster sauce and 'thousand-year' eggs. Chinese stone deities stand in service among precious silk textiles, teak tables and chairs, vintage photographs and an ancient Barong (*right*), the mythical creature of Balinese dance and drama, and mediator between good and evil.

ABOVE Vivid gold and reds are used throughout the ocean-view pavilion honouring Belgian artist Adrien Jean LeMayeur de Merpres. LeMayeur arrived in the early 1930s and fell in love with and married a beautiful Balinese *legong* dancer, Ni Polok. She is the model for many of his paintings, which depict daily life in Bali. Before her death in 1986, some furnishings and artworks from their Sanur home were purchased by Bapak Anhar.

LEFT Coral rock used in this exterior wall of the main lobby is indigenous to the *bukits* (hills) near Canggu village. Old, leaded stained-glass windows are from Java. The antique, stone balustrades set a tone of timelessness for this side entry into the hotel lobby.

ABOVE Carved wood panels, at least 100 years old, were collected in a small village in East Java and have been used to make a double-door side entry to the main lobby.

LEFT This water-therapy spa room has a tiled mural relating a legend of the dancing goddess Apsara: "My daughter, if your mind and soul are impure, and your life essence doesn't show on your skin, save some spare time, plunge your body into water and sprinkle yourself with the potpourri of 'The Blooming of the Universe'. Implore, and purification will flow into your skin, soul and your mind, jagad sumringah." — from a folksong (1706).

ABOVE This is the *Kamar Dandang Goela*, a mystical treatment room with Tibetan and Hindu influences. The massage tables are 100-year-old ironwood beds from Java; the space beneath them was used for storing valuables or rice. The decorative dragon rack was once used to hang the *gantungan* gamelan gong in Palace Two in Yogyakarta and is more than 200 years old. The wall hanging is a Tibetan *thanka* or mandala.

A beautiful Balinese woman waiting to greet guests arriving for a massage. The carved antique entrance doors are set into coral-rock walls. Lotus ponds and a garden are part of this private spa room with richly painted bamboo walls.

A vine-covered pergola leads to the white sandy beach of Canggu and the beautiful sea beyond.

OPPOSITE PAGE

TOP LEFT Service is private and personal at Hotel Tugu Bali. Old Javanese wooden beds by the pool have been converted for sunbathing; the storage areas beneath them were originally used for keeping valuables or rice.

TOP RIGHT Waroeng Tugu is where a light lunch or snacks of traditional Javanese food may be ordered anytime. Waroeng is the spelling from old Javanese language; the current spelling is warung. Cooking lessons take place here over wood-stoked fires, and traditional vessels and implements are used in preparing a full range of Javanese cuisine, bringing into the experience the strong, humble atmosphere of the Majapahit kingdom in Java and Bali hundreds of years ago. Handsome and rigid structure of king-post truss supports an authentic shingled roof. In the evenings, the warung is romantically lit with coconut oil lamps. Lucienne Anhar is seen in this photograph having lunch at one of the old warung tables.

BOTTOM LEFT This bale is where offerings for the hotel grounds and rooms are made; guests are welcome to join in and learn the art of making offerings. Here is a perfect example of the four-post bale, the archetypical structure of Balinese architecture which has been adapted for different purposes. The painting depicts a story about Arjuna, one of five Pandawa heroes from the Hindu epic, the Mahabharata.

BOTTOM RIGHT This little bale, sitting in the middle of a lotus pond, is the kamar solek or barbershop. Carved open filigree wall panels provide natural air-conditioning. Dated to between the late 18th- and 19th-century, the pavilion used to serve as the bed of a king from Madura Island.

THIS PAGE A bale for a warung jamoe (apothecary) where customized medicinal drinks are made from herbs and spices. Jamu (as the word is spelt today) ladies with their basket-backpack filled with bottles of liquid herbal remedies are a lovely sight in villages all over Bali and Java. Herbal remedies are still an important part of traditional medicine throughout the country.

Artisans of the village of Kamasan painted this imposing *kamasan* ceiling in the lobby of the Ritz-Carlton Bali.

Ritz-Carlton Bali

The Ritz-Carlton Bali hotel, in the village of Jimbaran, sits on a bluff overlooking the Indian Ocean on the southwestern coast of the island. The area is a dry coral hill where much of the limestone used on the island is quarried. Because of its close proximity to the international airport, Ngurah Rai, and beautiful white sand beaches, Jimbaran has become a favoured location for luxury hotels; all advertisements proclaiming magnificent Bali sunsets are completely understated.

The Ritz-Carlton Bali opened in late 1996 and was designed by architectural firm Wimberly, Allison, Tong & Good from Newport Beach, California (USA) in collaboration with P. T. Harapan Satria Tiga (Bali). Credit must be given to the owners, architects and designers for their willingness to integrate elements of traditional Balinese architecture into their planning. The hotel's *bale agung* lobby with a *kamasan* painting is a tribute to the village of Kamasan where this style of painting is an ancient tradition.

The art of *kamasan* painting *Kamasan* paintings are lavishly detailed narratives using classic *wayang*, or puppet-style figures, to tell rambling stories usually those from the *Mahabharata*. In the 18th century the raja of the village of Kamasan became the patron of this style, which is characterized by rich tones of red pigments on ochre backgrounds. This style flourished under his patronage. A treasure of old *kamasan* ceilings, some dating to around the 1700s, can still be seen in the buildings at the Taman Gili water garden floating pavilions complex in the town of Klungkung, in particular the old Hall of Justice building. In this pavilion, the paintings depict the horrors of war that befall wrongdoers. Walter Spies was involved in restoration work on these ceilings in the 1930s. A book by Idanna Pucci, *The Epic Of Life*, tells of the lessons to be learned from such paintings: "The accused, kneeling before the mighty tribunal, could not avoid the sight of the dreadful punishments depicted on the ceiling. But if he raised his eyes beyond, just a little above the horrors of Hell to the panels of Heaven, he could perhaps find some solace."

The open-air lobby has a spectacular view of the grounds, which includes swimming pools that step down to the Indian Ocean. *Bale* architecture has been used successfully to provide gathering places throughout the grounds; they are places where guests can meet, dine, lounge, play table tennis and enjoy the well-planned gardens. Landscape architects Sasaki Associates of Los Angeles, California (USA) utilized a variety of exotic trees including monkey pod, banyan, ironwood and several varieties of bamboo, resulting in gardens of interest and beauty. A bamboo-lined walkway leads bridal parties to the ocean-side glass chapel.

The guest villas of the Ritz-Carlton are tucked into the hills that overlook the ocean. Each has a thatched roof and limestone carvings set into walls and comes with a private garden. Interior furnishings include Indonesian teak furniture and textiles designed by Insada Interior Design Team from Jakarta.

It is the spectacular *wantilan* that shelters a Thalassos pool in the spa that captures one's full attention because of the exquisite construction of the traditional *alang-alang* thatch ceiling. The warm, organic colours of bamboo and thatch are a lovely contrast to the aqua blue water of this hydrotherapy pool.

The Ritz-Carlton represents the new resort architecture on Bali, blending modern elements with the old to remind guests of the traditions of this ancient island.

A dining *bale* floats in a pond overlooking the Indian Ocean—a perfect spot to enjoy sundown.

ABOVE LEFT Each village suite has a highly carved door leading from bedroom to sitting room. Exterior doors lead to a private plunge pool set within a walled garden.

ABOVE RIGHT Textures of the bamboo-thatched ceiling contrast superbly with the polished marble and rich *bengkerai* wood to make a luxurious bathroom for the village suite.

TOP LEFT The Aquatonic Thalossos pool holds 700 million litres of seawater and has 12 different exercise zones for advanced hydrotherapy. This pool sits under a large *wantilan bale agung*, sheltering it from sun and rain. The pool makes an oh-so-delightful, healthful gathering place.

BOTTOM LEFT Once the healing qualities of mineral-rich seawater has worked its magic, move over to the warm whirlpool located under a circular, double-tiered *bale* (*far right*).

ABOVE The only thing that is Balinese here is the beautiful landscape. This glass pavilion is a wedding chapel sitting on a bluff overlooking the Indian Ocean. Centre glass aisle is illuminated, through which one can see a stone-lined river flowing below. Sonnets full of metaphors could be written with this imagery: "Their lives flow together…oh never mind!"

TOP LEFT Strong rock buttresses around the pool area support *bale* for sunbathing. The waterfall effect is not only lovely to look at but also pleasant to the ears. The sound is refreshing, as is swimming through and sitting under the splash.

MIDDLE An antique entry gate with Chinese elements opens to a dining and poolside bar area.

BOTTOM Slate wall has a limestone air-vent delicately hand-carved in a floral design. The combination is a yin and yang of colour and material.

ABOVE Lush tropical foliage and the gentle sounds of water along winding paths and stairs line the way to the Ritz-Carlton Bali Spa, bringing guests into a calm and meditative state-of-being. Coral-rock wall, dark river stones and natural bamboo hand-rail make a handsome composition of contrasting colours and materials.

ABOVE Welcome to the spa at the Ritz where they tell no evil, see no evil and hear no evil. Playful bronze monkeys make a humorous graphic outdoor sculpture. The traditional bamboo lattice on the thatch roof is a device used for anchoring the *alang-alang* in windy locations.

LEFT Carved polychrome entry gates to each villa sets the tone for a distinctive Bali style. Each gate is topped with a thatched roof. Crossing the threshold leads you to a private water and flower garden.

ABOVE Surrounding the dining rooms of Laka Leke are lotus ponds and garden views to one side and *sawah* fields to the other. It is a restaurant gathering place to experience Balinese life in a rural setting.

OPPOSITE Entertainment at Laka Leke includes watching the rice being planted or harvested, or the *sawah* being prepared. On this rainy day, preparation of the *sawah* for planting must go forward as auspicious days have been determined for when the planting cycle should begin. Cows on Bali are well taken care of; they have a daily bath and grass is cut and brought to their bamboo shelter within the family compound. The owners of Laka Leke continue the traditional methods of farming in an effort to keep the Balinese culture alive and to give visitors the chance to be in close contact with the rural side of the island.

RESTAURANTS

Laka Leke

Laka Leke in the Balinese language means 'hidden place'… and hidden indeed describes the restaurant Laka Leke, although it is only minutes away from busy Ubud. The restaurant, located in the quiet, rural village of Nyuh Kuning, sits on the edge of a *sawah*, a working wet-rice field. The concept for Laka Leke grew out of designer Mande Sudarta's desire to honour the rice fields and rice goddess Dewi Sri as well as the traditions of rice cultivation that are integral in the lives of the Balinese.

Using this ideal, Mande developed a concept for dining pavilions using the shape of the traditional rice granary, the *lumbung*. Each dining *bale* is a raised platform supported by structural coconut-tree posts. Roofs of *alang-alang* are shaped in the familiar upside down boat shape of a traditional *lumbung*.

According to Mande: "*Lumbung* in family compounds are built high off the ground to protect the rice from rodents and have sharply sloping roofs, rounded slightly at the ridge, to keep off as much water as possible. The ground area under the rice storage portion of the *lumbung* is a place where men gathered in rainy weather to socialize, gamble and drink a little *arak* (palm wine)." This gathering place aspect of *lumbung* design gave Mande the idea that dining pavilions should have *lesehan*-style dining—sitting on floor cushions. The immensely beautiful and ever-changing landscape of the *sawah* provides an unequaled panorama for diners as they recline on floor pillows surrounding low dining tables. For those not wanting to recline as they feast, there are dining pavilions with chairs and tables.

Mande is brother to owners Ibu Wayan and Ketut Krinting. Ibu Wayan is a distinguished chef, well-known throughout Europe, Australia and the United States as an extraordinary culinarian of the Balinese cuisine. She is the founder and owner of Café Wayan on Monkey Forest Road in Ubud, a gathering place for tourists and locals since 1986. The restaurant is recognized in Indonesia as one of Bali's most outstanding and has also received accolades from around the world.

Laka Leke continues Ibu Wayan's famous style that is known for creative and delicious quality Indonesian food. Mande, however, is adding interest beyond the fabulous food; he is designing new programmes that support Balinese culture: "My earnest hope is to help the people of Bali keep their culture alive and to share the culture with visitors." He is reinstating the old methods of organic rice farming to the *sawah* that surrounds the restaurant. They are growing the original long-grain Bali rice as well as a wide range of vegetables demanded by the varied menu of the restaurant. He hopes that by setting

this standard, others on Bali will be encouraged to return to organic farming.

As manager and director of the organic farming programme at Laka Leke, Mande organizes the work of cultivation to take place during peak dining hours; this provides an entertaining as well as educational sight for diners. Set against the backdrop of the *sawah* and depending on the season, one can see farmers turning the soil for yet another cycle of planting or harvesting rice or bundling rice into sheaths or even ducks cleaning up after a harvest.

If you happen to arrive at Laka Leke on a Monday night or the night of a full moon, you will be enthralled by the Kecek and Fire Dance, a traditional trance dance that is performed by 100 men. These dance performances, supported by Laka Leke, are performed once a week by local people from Nyuh Kuning and Peliatan villages. There is always a special happening every day at this restaurant, one that serves up a close view of the culture of Bali along with some of the best food on the island.

ABOVE Planting the *sawah* is done by men while harvesting is the work of women. Both men and women tend the *padi*, cleaning and nurturing the rice during the growth cycle. Having lunch in the dining *bale* are Ibu Wayan and Mande Sudarta.

LEFT Ketut Krinting, one of the owners of Laka Leke, herds ducks into a recently harvested *sawah*; the ducks clean the fields of insects as well as bits of grain that might have been left behind after the harvest.

TOP LEFT This traditional landscape painting with the canvas completely filled with scenes of rural Bali is a superb painting by Ketut Krinting… yes, the same man herding ducks and an owner of Laka Leke. The owners and managers of Laka Leke are all multi-talented. Ibu Wayan is a chef extraordinaire, Ketut is an accomplished painter, and Mande Sudarta (Ibu Wayan's brother) is a talented designer.

TOP RIGHT Now that the padi has grown, the dining pavilions float in a sea of green. The *lumbung* pavilion with round-shaped roof (*right*) is a fine adaptation of this traditional form. The rectangular pavilion is a typical *bale*.

LEFT Men from the villages of Nyuh Kuning and Peliatan dance the Kecak dance under the full moon at Laka Leke, part of the Purnama Bulan ceremonies held once a month, and on every Monday night.

ABOVE LEFT Like a tropical loggia, the entry lounge area of the restaurant weaves a spell of quiet, sensual enchantment.

ABOVE RIGHT The signpost to the restaurant is a handsome representation of designs used in *lamak* offering panels, which are dedicated to the rice goddess Dewi Sri. Artist and metal worker, Pintor Sirait, designed and executed all the wrought copper and steel components in the restaurant.

BOTTOM Worked wrought metal in this open kitchen has an unusual airy quality and continues the *lamak* theme.

OPPOSITE Large etched glass panels in pivoting metal doors open to a private lounge and wine room. The light fixture has a linen shade hand-painted with a *kamasan* painting.

Lamak Restaurant

There are plenty of distractions as one walks along busy Monkey Forest Road in Ubud. However, an artfully executed sign in wrought copper with the word 'Lamak' on it demands attention and begs investigation. Taking the few steps up from the sidewalk level is a delightful surprise, for here is a smartly designed restaurant that relies on familiar components of traditional Balinese architecture such as bamboo, *alang-alang* thatch roofs and richly polished teak woods. Together with the innovative use of steel and wrought copper designs, a stage is set for upscale dining in Ubud.

The entrance is a long, narrow gallery of a room, like a tropical loggia with comfortable lounge chairs covered in contemporary patterned fabrics and a high-gabled ceiling of *alang-alang* resting on dark wood rafters. The narrowness of the gallery and the exposed structural components of a high ceiling accentuates this dramatic entry, directing the focus to a garden dining area straight ahead. There is a conflict of emotions; there is at once a desire to drop into the very inviting chairs in the lounge area, yet rush ahead to the very romantic setting of the dining courtyard. Stylized *lamak* designs are featured as decorative elements throughout the restaurant—in the balcony railings of the upper dining area, on the steel veneer covering the half-wall opening into the kitchen and on doors and hardware fittings. Contrasting with the hardness of copper and steel are large panels of richly stained polished wood louvres, tropical foliage and low-level lighting.

There is an exciting spatial interaction between the different dining and lounge areas; it is a pleasant mingling of space, patterns and textural organic materials as these components meet head-on with sophisticated dining. At the restaurant, there is a successful combination of what could have been conflicting intentions if not for the artistic skill and eye of the owners and the design team of Made Wijaya (Michael White). Together they have created an elegant restaurant with tropical flair using traditional Balinese materials up-styled by the addition of sleek, artistically wrought metal design elements.

LaLuciola Restaurant

Gentle sea breezes blow through the huge two-level canopy of LaLuciola Restaurant, providing natural air-conditioning even on the hottest day in tropical, equatorial Bali. LaLuciola is on Kayu Aya beach, near Seminyak, and is one of the prettiest beaches in all of Bali.

The butterfly-roof is completely open on the front façade of the two-storey spaces of LaLuciola, certainly a reach of the traditional design of a *bale agung wantilan* but nevertheless an exciting adaptation for a place to dine and the food is equally exciting.

Diners at LaLuciola frequently have the privilege of a view never to be forgotten… that of a sacred procession of Balinese in full ceremonial dress walking along the water's edge with accompanying gamelan gongs sounding harmonic rhythms as the orange tropical setting sun dips into the sea.

OPPOSITE This colourful, beach-side tropical garden dining area is at the sand level of the grand pavilion at LaLuciola.

ABOVE The open-air pavilion at LaLuciola, on the beach near Seminyak, is sheltered by an umbrella of *alang-alang* and bamboo. The beach area near the restaurant is a sacred area so diners can frequently watch processions of seaside ceremonies.

LEFT Way up high at the very top of the ceiling, it is possible to see the roof's magnificent design in bamboo and thatch. Here, a stepped wood decorative feature seen in Balinese architecture is used to bring the rafters to a single point. If diners happen to look up, they will see a menagerie of very healthy bats and a *cecek*, or small lizard. Bali is a place of living close to nature. With open-air pavilions, creatures can easily fly in and out and are not the problem they may be when rooms are enclosed.

Indus Restaurant

Indus Restaurant sits at the top of the ravine looking down to the Wos River as it runs down to the village of Campuhan, near Ubud. It is a beautiful view and one that complements the fine menu and good food that the restaurant serves up. Designed by owners Ketut Suardana and Janet deNeefe, the same couple also own and run Honeymoon Homestay nearby. Janet's creative menu includes Balinese and Indonesian dishes, sometimes with a slight twist that caters to an international palate.

ABOVE Alcoves at Indus Restaurant are inviting places to gather while drinking in the amazing views of rivers and mountains. The underside of the *alang-alang* thatch and bamboo roof is rustic and provides an interesting textural mix with the stylized Ionic columns. A tall shrine stands in the sacred northeast corner of the restaurant.

OPPOSITE TOP Staff of the restaurant arrive early to make *canang*, woven baskets for offerings to be placed on tables, in the kitchen and just about everywhere else, delighting the eye with their carefully constructed beauty. The columns and supporting structural work are reminiscent of Dutch colonial architecture; however, here they are given a light and playful treatment.

OPPOSITE BOTTOM The view from the verandah looks to the ridge where *alang-alang* is grown for thatch roofs while the ridges beyond are terraced with rice fields. Lemon grass, a favoured spice in Balinese cuisine, is grown in pots for decoration on the verandah.

KuDeTa Restaurant

Everyone who is anyone in Bali's expatriate community shows up for sunset and cocktails at KuDeTa. As the shadows lengthen, the island's cognoscenti drift onto the bar's breezy beachfront deck, their linen shirts billowing open to expose native jewellery, their Thai fisherman's pants revealing calves tanned and toned by long walks on Kuta beach. A dj spins his latest chill mix, the international assemblage settles into chaise longues and the sun plunges into the Bali Strait. It's the typical end to a typical day in Seminyak.

— feature writer Wayne Arnold for the New York Times

KuDeTa is just as reported; this restaurant's Bali-chic design and tasty food have captured a continental set of loyal customers from the nearby beach areas of Kuta. Ubud loyalists are often seen there as well. With the turn of the millennium, architecture in Bali has captured a new vitality to match a virtual reality world of electronic technology connecting tourists travelling from most corners of the world. The design at KuDeTa has stepped into this new century with its modern interior and is an influencing direction for a change of architectural style on Bali. KuDeTa's design was the result of collaborative efforts by architect Frederic (Fredo) Tassin and owner Arthur Chondro's Australian business, Nine Squares Development Co. They chose *batu candi* stone from central Java as a decorative material for the bar, walls, exterior floors, stairs and in their well-designed public restrooms. *Candi* stone, together with beautiful *merbau* wood, are used as flooring in the main pavilion. The restaurant's furniture was made in Indonesia.

OPPOSITE Grey *candi* stone tiles face the front and sides of the well-designed bar above which hang painted bamboo pendant lamps. Ambient lighting is provided inconspicuously throughout the restaurant through the recesses in concrete columns. Wood decorative grid inserted into the concrete beam is an open design that allows for ventilation.

TOP LEFT The main dining area of KuDeTa features dynamic components of traditional Balinese ceilings, setting a tone for the strong visual elements of load-bearing concrete columns and endwalls. Boxy teak wood and upholstered furniture continue the robust contemporary interior. *Merbau*-wood floors repeat the colouration of the ceiling and provide an elegant, warm contrast to an otherwise very contemporary space.

ABOVE Polished grey *candi* stone from Java on the counter top and bar-face interact perfectly with art deco-like teak bar stools. Red-lacquered bamboo light cylinders make a handsome contemporary contrast to Bali's organic foliage.

BOTTOM The reflecting pond is a gathering place for children to play on weekends as their parents lounge at the bar or on the beachfront. KuDeTa's main dining room and surrounding bar lounge areas feel completely open to the outside.

Public gathering
places of modern Bali

LEFT Small bamboo *pondok* such as this one can be seen throughout the *sawah*, placed here and there for workers to rest, take their tea and mid-day meals while exchanging current news. The raised platform design follows the traditional form of *bale*.

ABOVE *Wantilan* at Pura Penetaran Sasih, Pejeng. This is a fine example of traditional Balinese *wantilan* architecture. King-post trusses at the very top support the first tier of the *alang-alang* roof. The second tier begins just below the clerestory, which allows hot air trapped in the structure to escape. *Wantilan* at temples such as this provide a space for villagers to assemble special shrines for use in temple ceremonies; to perform music, dance and drama during temple ceremonies as well as to gather for ritual cockfights. *Wantilan* in villages are social halls for *banjar* meetings to discuss village affairs and for gamelan musicians or dance troupes to practise. Since the democratization of Indonesia, they also serve as polling stations.

The gathering places of modern Bali are often places without architectural structures, since Bali remains 'an outdoor living place'. It is in the culture of the people to live outside, to be in the open courtyards of temples or in the family compound where social gatherings have only the sky as a roof.

In Denpasar, there is a large public park that has become a Sunday afternoon place for families to gather; even the grounds around the gargantuan statue of Arjuna on the by-pass road from the airport has become a meeting place for teenagers. *Wantilan*, or open-air social halls, are also the gathering place of choice for people living in the largest town to the smallest village. Bamboo *pondok,* those small *bale* dotted among the rice fields, are other gathering places where workers get together for a break from their work; they are also where people can meet in unusually beautiful settings to quietly pass the news. In some of the larger towns, *warung* have become the place for young people to 'hang out', but in the villages they remain a place for all to stop and chat while having a spicy snack and a hot cup of tea or Bali *kopi*.

Some gathering places that might be considered national infrastructure in other countries are being supported at the local *banjar* level in Bali. For example, libraries are being built with the help of the local people and school facilities are being improved by the parents of the children. Frank Olcvary, director of Bali Hati organization, set a precedent in the village of Penestanan when he organized a parents' committee to oversee funds that were given to improve the basic facilities of its elementary school. New desks were bought, computers were donated and the school grounds upgraded. Many villages today have improvement programmes for their schools and these are run by a dedicated *banjar* group.

Indonesia is still a developing country, a nation with more than 238 million people of which 30 percent of those are under 15 years old. This expansive country is not a continent but an archipelago of thousands of islands on which more than 300 ethnic groups live. Indonesia has tremendous resources in not only minerals and other commodities but also in its indigenous people, who are industrious and entrepreneurial by nature. It is a country of great potential but it has faced incredibly difficult situations in trying to resolve political and infrastructure issues with so many different islands that are spread over a large area.

The people of Bali, however, have the advantage of possessing a naturally positive attitude that values the importance of being responsible for their own well-being. As a result, the Balinese are moving ahead and making tremendous strides towards bettering their lives. They also have the advantage of having both local Balinese leaders and an expatriate community who care greatly about the island and who work together to tackle local problems.

* *The Balinese language is onomatopoeic; consequently, the Balinese word for 'cricket' cemereret is the same as the sound they make. Similarly, the word for 'frog' is grobog and is pronounced just like a large bullfrog sounds, with a long-rolled 'r'.*

AGUNG RAI MUSEUM OF ART

This museum is about God's art and man-made art.

— Agung Rai, Founder and Director
Agung Rai Museum of Art (ARMA)

As a 20-year-old, Agung Rai dreamed about building a museum with a difference, one that would feature not only paintings but one that would actively sponsor and promote the cultural arts of Bali: "I spent twelve years selling paintings on Kuta beach just to earn money and buy land to build a museum, a museum with nature's art in the form of plants and trees, especially those for medicine; where one can see nature's art in the *sawah*—padi art. It would be a museum that could help keep the traditions of *budaya* (custom) alive through paintings, music and dance."

Agung Rai's dream is now a reality. His museum, the Agung Rai Museum of Art (ARMA) in Pengosekan in Ubud, is a treasure in itself. The museum has compelling visuals not only in its collection of paintings and sculpture from different periods in Bali's history but in its buildings and gardens. A visit is a delight to all the senses: a walk in the gardens allows you to see and smell the sweet scent of exotic plants and trees and hear the rushing sounds of the *subak* waters against a background of crickets singing *cemerereret-cemerereret**. Add these to the sounds of children learning to dance and play the gamelan instruments, cows and roosters uttering their usual vocals, and you get a full cacophony of sounds that meld into a hum of peacefulness.

The museum provides a gathering place for visitors to observe traditional Balinese dance and drama. While its architecture reflects Bali's traditions in design, its open-stage performances keep alive the rich Balinese tradition of music and dance.

This entry bridge leads visitors from the main building of the museum to exhibit halls set amongst beautiful gardens of flowering old frangipani trees, champaka trees and ginger plants.

Each month, the Purnama Bulan (full moon) ceremony is a rare treat featuring various artistic performances. Each week young Balinese attend classes in the traditional arts at no charge; the only requirement is a desire to learn and participate. Other aspects of the museum, such as the cultural workshops it organizes as well as the museum library and its archives, work to educate and deepen the understanding of the Balinese culture, as do the paintings from the permanent collections and the revolving temporary exhibits. The museum and its grounds embody Bali's rich cultural heritage and reflect the principles of *adat*, *budaya* and *agama*.

The museum, which is located within walking range of Ubud, also provides accommodation for visitors to allow them to experience the full range of the activities it organizes. Whether it is a standard room or a walled villa, all rooms are set in a serene environment within the museum grounds. The upkeep of the museum is supported by the ARMA Resort and its three restaurants on the grounds, by the sale of art at the Agung Rai Gallery in Peliatan and by the ARMA Foundation. Worldwide conferences such as the Conference for World Peace are part of the on-going activities at the museum.

Agung Rai is living his dream of a cultural museum through the ARMA. He hopes "to pass on to Balinese children the spirit of Walter Spies' sensibility to the arts, to raise up their vibration of who they are, why they are here and where they are from, to appreciate the artistic aura of nature and see nature as a source of inspiration". As he says:

> *Bali is so small yet has a magnetic and holy ingredient from China and India; the altruistic power and magic of Bali cannot be felt from rationale. Complex Bali is a conflict of the metaphysical and the rationale. Here we have not just a museum, it is an ashram— inspiration comes from just sitting. You create yourself from the interaction of a human with nature and nature with a human. We need to be more aware to feed our soul. [It is] easy to feed our stomach, but the soul remains hungry.*

OPPOSITE TOP Detail of a *paras* stone panel on a building at the museum.

OPPOSITE BOTTOM Agung Rai regularly meets visitors to the museum. He is always willing to discuss the subjects he loves most—art, nature and Balinese culture.

ABOVE LEFT A group of gallery and accessory buildings at ARMA are of a style developed in the 1980s and seen in large government buildings, universities and museums. Some Dutch colonial holdover can be seen juxtaposed with highly decorative Balinese architectural elements.

ABOVE SanSan opens a gold-leaf door leading into a main gallery building of the Agung Rai Museum of Art. The door is set in a highly carved entryway of red Bali brick and *paras* stone carvings.

BOTTOM This painting, by I. Wayan Pendet (1936), depicts men and women forming an elephant. It is a fascinating study with intriguing imagery and intricate patterns. Measuring 100 cm by 150 cm, it is part of the collection of the ARMA Foundation.

ABOVE A dynamic ceiling caps the main gallery of the museum, which spans two storeys. The paintings in this gallery show a progression of Balinese art through different periods. The large *kamasan* painting on the far right (artist unknown), entitled *Kerebut Kumbakarma*, tells of a story from the *Ramayana*. Large *kamasan* paintings, framed in multi-hued carved wood, also surround the upper walls of the atrium skylights.

TOP RIGHT White roof trusses make a dynamic contrast to the dark polished wood rafters and *bedeg* (woven bamboo matting) ceiling. On the far wall is a painting titled, "Between Heaven & Earth" (2002) by Dutch artist Walter Van Oel, who lives in Sanur. The large painting in the centre of the recess on the right is "Upacara-upacara Puri di Bali (Temple Ceremony in Bali)" (1933) by P. N. Wardhana.

BOTTOM RIGHT Warung Kopi is one of three restaurants at the museum. The unusual design on the post is made from pieces of *paras* stone. Ceiling detail shows the red *tali* (string) often used in traditional *alang-alang* ceilings to tie the grass shingles to the bamboo rafters.

Guest rooms are available on the museum grounds for those who wish to immerse themselves in Balinese culture. Here is a standard room with resting *bale* overlooking the gardens. Golden bamboo adds a beautiful contrast to the green foliage of the Balinese gardens.

TOP LEFT The handsome proportions of the *angkul*, or gate, make for an inviting entry to one of the guest villas at the museum.

TOP RIGHT Lotus ponds surround each of the walled villa suites. Each villa comes with a 'floating' *bale* to relax and contemplate the art of nature in Bali.

ABOVE The upper floor of one of the private villas has a room for meditation. Carved, polychrome panels depict the white herons that flock to the nearby Petulu village. The window looks out to nature and the green *sawah* speckled with white herons on the lookout for eel and snails.

LEFT The bedrooms of the villa suites have polished teak floors and most of the furniture is teak. Agung Rai and his wife designed the interiors of all the villas and guest rooms.

RIGHT These girls are ready for class to begin, hair still wet from their morning bath, fresh flowers tucked into their ponytails, neatly pressed sarongs and elastic waist belt in place. But wait a moment… now what might the personality be of that little girl rocking back on her blue platform sandals?

BOTTOM LEFT A weekly dance class in session at the museum. Here, world-famous Balinese dancer Ni Gusti Raka (see her life story in the book *Dancing Out of Bali*) instructs young girls and boys on the techniques of Balinese dance, a complicated dance form that requires the eyes, arms, torso, feet, hands, fingers and mind to be all engaged. Children training under Ibu Raka, a national treasure in Indonesia's arts scene, are fortunate to have this chance to learn from the master.

BOTTOM RIGHT Young Balinese girls learning to dance at the museum. The beauty and liveliness of the Balinese people are seen in this young girl—smooth bronze skin; trim body wearing a colourful, modern and somewhat whimsical sarong; her lovely face serenely involved in the task of the moment. She is one of many young women who will step out into the future with a firm background in her culture.

BALI HATI

In all of its activities, the Bali Hati projects aim to be a living example of how we all can function from the centre of our hearts and how we can find our power there.

— *Frank Olcvary, Founder and Director of Bali Hati*

Hati means 'heart' in the Indonesian language, and the name suggests that the heart—the beauty of Bali—is its people. Bali Hati represents a modern concept of a gathering place for Balinese, a place to gather to learn about oneself and to experience a community outreach programme.

The Bali Hati projects vary in focus but not in principle. Established in 1997, they are designed to help young Balinese men and women realize their individual and social potential through education and the provision of social welfare services.

Frank Olcvary explains his concept of the project and the mission of Bali Hati: "The underlying intent is to create an environment where love and concern, combined with educational and social initiatives, can achieve not only spiritual and intellectual growth of individuals but can ultimately bring about fundamental changes in their economic and social life. Community service is viewed as an important part of this learning experience. Although Bali Hati recognizes and tries to reinforce the close interrelationship of spiritual, intellectual and material achievement, it is in no way associated with any religious foundation, sect or denomination and has no political affiliation; we must remain autonomous to achieve the greatest possible potential."

OPPOSITE The entrance to Spa Hati winds past lotus ponds and rice fields. Proceeds from the operation of Spa Hati go towards the Taman Hati Elementary School programme.

ABOVE Glass blocks filter the warm tropical sun into the massage rooms. The grounds are a sanctuary of stillness, with lotus ponds, natural trickling water sounds and soft muted colours.

LEFT A massage *bale* floats on a sea of green.

ABOVE This massage room for two is filled with natural light from the skylights and glass-block walls. Vents above the walls are open to allow air to flow through. Carvings are on *paras* stone, all from Bali. Whirlpool tub and shower area complete this inviting massage room. The pebble-filled border inset in the marble floors form an attractive detail and serves as a drain.

LEFT Professional massage treatments at Spa Hati are followed by a sauna session and whirlpool saltwater soak. Heavenly! The stone wall of the whirlpool area is built of attractive aqua stones from Java. The hand-carved vent is made of *paras* stone.

Some of the organization's current projects include:

Rumah Hati This is a community centre and mini conference centre with facilities for workshop training, a free library for children and a community swimming pool. There are plans to build a larger community library once funds become available.

Kertha Hati This is a free law consultation programme for people who cannot afford legal services to solve personal issues such as family disputes and land rights. Kertha Hati also advises Balinese women on their legal rights based on the *adat* (customary law) as well as assists in mediation between villages for general disputes. When court action is necessary, Kertha Hati looks for volunteer lawyers to provide free representation.

Taman Hati Kindergarten and Elementary School Started in 1999 in Mas village near Ubud, this school offers children the best possible education using a variety of creative teaching methods such as the Montessori and Steiner methods. Children attending this school are mostly from families in need of economic help, although there is also a broad spectrum of students from families with varying degrees of situations. These students pay tuition to help the operating costs of Taman Hati. Not only that, their presence provides a healthy social mix in classes.

Bali Hati Volleyball This volleyball team was formed as part of an effort to publicize the work of Bali Hati. The privately sponsored team has done well in area tournaments.

Satya Hati Satya Hati is the name of a pop music band that became the inspiration for a new music programme. It was formed when members of a band from a neighbouring town came to the Bali Hati offices and said, "We have no work and don't want to drink alcohol or use drugs." With musical equipment provided by private sponsors, the band performs monthly concerts in local communities; people who are now drug-free give a short talk about the negative effects drugs had on their lives at these sessions.

The entry doors to classrooms at Taman Hati Elementary School are traditional with panels hand-carved in teak. Rattan racks are for the placement of sandals before students enter classrooms. Ceiling is made of *bedeg* on wood rafters.

In addition to all these programmes, Bali Hati runs the Medical Mobile Clinic and has given tremendous support and assistance to those who have suffered trauma and injury from accidents. Bali Hati has also initiated government-school renovation projects that involve organizing villages and sponsors to provide labour and funds to install electricity and running water for bathrooms and tiles for flooring, to carry out roof repairs, and to donate or sponsor supplies, teaching aids, computers, desks and other equipment.

To support the running of the Taman Hati kindergarten and elementary school, a spa was opened behind the Bali Hati office complex near Ubud. All profits from Spa Hati—an oasis of luxurious pampering that includes massage room, steam room, outdoor saltwater whirlpool, a fitness room and lap pool—go towards supporting the school. The Bali Hati office building has an educational complex with classrooms where the locals can go for courses in English and computer skills. Ngurah Bagadia is a lawyer and operational director and Wayan Arnaya, the first Bali Hati student to have completed his university training, is associate director.

OPPOSITE Two large *wantilan*-style pavilions at Rumah Hati provide space for children to read, listen to lectures and gather for special events. The buildings are gathering places for seminars and workshops for communities. Stark white concrete posts and beams contrast sharply with the organic wood and *bedeg* ceilings.

ABOVE "Wheee! Let's go swimming at the Rumah Hati pool." The whistle blows and the group waiting jumps in while those swimming move out to wait another turn. According to Wayan Wira, the director of Rumah Hati (lifeguard in red and white), more than 100 children come three days each week for swimming lessons and to use its library facilities.

TOP LEFT On Bali, sandals are never worn inside a house or shop but are always left at the entrance, and even here at the entry gate to the Rumah Hati pool.

MIDDLE The Bali Hati logo consists of two figures happily dancing with their hearts open—a clear comparison to the heart-oriented efforts of the Bali Hati organization. The logo is part of a wall constructed with *paras* stone from the village of Taro in north Bali.

BOTTOM This colourful library at Rumah Hati offers Balinese children a place to read and a chance to use computers after a swim in the community pool.

BALI PURNATI CENTRE

*Bali Purnati Centre is dedicated to the preservation,
promotion, presentation and creation of new directions in
the performing, visual and design arts.*

— *Wayan Wartini, General Manager*

The word *purnati* in the Balinese language means 'a whole or pure heart' and it is from this word that the Bali Purnati Centre gets its name. Located in the Penataran *desa* near the town of Batuan-Sukawati, an area known for diverse classical and contemporary art forms, this conference centre is a gathering place for artists, writers, musicians and film-makers from within Indonesia and around the world to meet, discuss, create. Seminar and workshop attendees often put up performances for the benefit of the general public.

The Wos River, one of Bali's sacred rivers, meanders through a lush ravine at the back of the property. Overlooking this beautiful ravine is a performance amphitheatre with stepped seating that takes advantage of the natural contours of the land and the terracing of an old *sawah*. A *padmasana* temple, a shrine to the Sun god Surya, is near the amphitheatre.

The social centre of Purnati is its large open-air pavilion that seems to float above the river. This *wantilan*-style structure is a perfect design for the varied activities of the arts centre. This open-air space has a wonderful wood floor for dance or other rehearsals and is an ideal spot for conducting workshops. The *paras* stone building beneath it houses other amenities such as conference rooms, exhibition space, multi-purpose rooms, a library and a kitchen.

Bali Purnati Centre is a gathering place where international artists can find comfortable facilities that support and provide a variety of work environments. Here they can have a group retreat to study and to create many multi-disciplined activities. Accommodation is available in the form of *lumbung* built in the gardens, which give visitors an opportunity to experience living in a bamboo-and-thatch roofed Balinese-style accommodation.

TOP Bali Purnati Centre's 'floating' pavilion is also used for seminars, meetings and dinners. The site steps down to the Wos River; this natural crevasse in the terrain became a design feature that has provided a dramatic entry for this main building.

BOTTOM The tiered seating of the amphitheatre follows the original terraced landscape of the *sawah*. *Batu candi*, a dark stone from Java, was used for the stage and seating.

RIGHT This *lumbung* is one of the accommodations provided for conference participants who wish to stay on the grounds of the arts centre.

OPPOSITE Making a strong architectural statement—*paras* stone walls of meeting rooms, exhibition space and kitchen form a strong foundation and a pleasing contemporary contrast to the traditional open-air *wantilan* on the upper floor. The entry wood deck is actually a bridge across the *subak* waters that flow from one property to the next. Lily ponds and a *lingga-yoni* stone sculpture are the focal points from the entry.

ABOVE Extraordinarily handsome detailing of this *bale* follows elements seen in traditional Balinese architecture. This *bale* is near the swimming pool and is used for lounging around or for conference attendees to hold meetings in an informal setting.

LEFT The snack bar at Bali Purnati Centre is located in a fine little *bale* with closed walls on two sides.

Elements of
design

LANDSCAPE AS ARCHITECTURE

Rhythmic patterns of the richly coloured and textured rice terraces step up and down the slopes of Bali. Each terrace is carved into the hill, grooved to match the movement of the slope, each succeeding step reverberating a sensual rhythm. The sea of emerald green *sawah* reflects a rhythm, a patterning that has been embodied and celebrated in the arts and architecture of Bali.

The use of repeated and continuous patterns found in Balinese architecture and the other arts may well have evolved from the *sawah* landscapes and Bali's rice culture. Recorded history reveals that rice cultivation on the island has existed for at least ten centuries. A combination of warm and wet weather, fertile volcanic soil and the industrious nature of the Balinese have resulted in an agrarian society that harmonizes its human needs with nature. The endeavour of tilling the soil has established an honesty of life, while the cycle of harvest visually re-enacts life's cycle of birth and rebirth. This small island has been tenderly shaped for centuries, giving rise to the textured, green terraced *sawah* that today gives Bali the appearance of a life-sized topographical map.

The repeated, stepped sequence of movement in the landscape of the *sawah* is a rhythmic theme in all of the Balinese arts, regardless of whether it is in the brick coursings on walls or entry gates, or in the repeated rhythms of traditional music.

A design element that has evolved from Bali's rice culture and one that is much loved by the Balinese is the *tjili*, a native Balinese design found in all of the arts. *Tjili* represents the 'rice mother', who is either Dewi Sri (the wife of Wisnu and the goddess of agriculture, fertility and success who represents all that is good and beautiful) or Dewi Melanting (the daughter of Dewi Sri and the goddess of seeds and plants). According to legend, Dewi Melanting spends half of the year in the soil and the other half above ground. Says Dr R. Goris, writer and archaeologist dedicated to studying Balinese culture: "She [Dewi Melanting] has first to undergo death under the black earth before she can come to new life".

Nature, rhythm, drama, beauty and cycles of repetition. These are basic themes in Balinese art and culture and in everyday living, all drawn richly from Bali's rice culture and beautiful landscape. Repetition and pattern have become part of the Balinese spirit, the inner self that finds its expression in its architecture and in the performing arts. However serene the Balinese culture seems to be, a paradox exists behind its many layers—that of busyness. The mild-mannered Balinese living in harmony with nature contrast sharply to the way they express themselves in their art, dance and architecture. Most Balinese lead simple lives in the spartan comfort of their homes, which are a study in simplicity. Yet when they attend temple ceremonies, they dress in exquisitely designed fabrics adorned with gold and brocade. Similarly, while the temple courtyards are bare, temple gates are constructed with multi-depth brick courses interrupted with ornately carved mystical animals or floral tendrils. This explains why temple ceremonies in the humblest of villages are still a mesmerizing complexity of visual beauty: dance, drama, rich clothing, beautifully constructed offerings—all of these take place against an exuberantly embellished architectural backdrop upon a bare dirt floor. This contradiction is further intensified with the crashing crescendo of complicated gamelan orchestra rhythms and sounds. All are presented with great flourish creating a sensually dramatic air that contrasts with the light, effervescent nature of the Balinese who refuse to take life too seriously. Their lives have an unaffected grandeur.

OPPOSITE An old wall with relief depicting a procession shows the busyness and complexities that define the Balinese style of living.

ABOVE Terraced *sawah*, a flowing sea of green, with bamboo *pondok* scattered through the rice fields. These are little places for gathering and resting, an organic architectural gathering place for rice field workers.

Rice, the principal source of life The Balinese treat rice with reverence and respect; it is their nourishment, their sustenance of life. Rice is considered a gift from Wisnu, the god of water and fertility. An allegorical legend tells of Wisnu coming down to earth to impregnate Mother Earth so that the people would have more than just sugarcane juice for food. That fertilization of the earth—recognized as a cosmic and divine act of female and male creative forces that are represented in water and earth—gave birth to rice by way of the patron god of the South, Sanghyang Kesuhum Kidul, who then sent four doves bearing seeds that represent the four cardinal colours. Thus the symbolic concept of the *sanga mandala* (a spiritual compass with colour and direction determining spiritual orientation) is integrated into this legend with white, black and red varieties of rice. As there is no yellow variety of rice, the spice turmeric is cooked with white rice to provide the desired brilliant yellow.

Most visitors to Bali are surprised and amazed at the constant occupation of the Balinese in their daily affairs and with the busyness in the artistic expression of their culture. Even Noel Coward's short poem to Charlie Chaplin during their visit to Bali accents these thoughts:

> *As I said this morning to Charlie*
> *There is far too much music in Bali,*
> *And although as a place it's entrancing,*
> *There is also a thought too much dancing.*
> *It appears that each Balinese native,*
> *From the womb to the tomb is creative,*
> *And although the results are quite clever,*
> *There is too much artistic endeavour*
>
> — *Adrian Vickers,* Bali: A Paradise Created
> *Credited to Frank Clune,* The Isles Of Spice *(1940)*

The Balinese busily go about their daily lives. Women seem to never have idle hands and moments of relaxation are spent weaving small baskets for the daily offerings. Men and women share the responsibility of preparing ceremonial offerings. Meanwhile, the rice fields need tending, dance and music must be rehearsed, the *banjar* meetings must be attended, the temple needs cleaning—all these in addition to raising a family or attending to a regular day job. A definite busyness permeates the island and yet the Balinese always have time to stop and visit. They never seem rushed or frantic; there is time to take. Amidst this chaotic busyness, however, there is a sense of serenity. Miguel Covarrubias got it so poetically right in *Island of Bali*:

> *Like a continual under-sea ballet, the pulse of life in Bali*
> *moves with a measured rhythm reminiscent of the sway*
> *of marine plants and the flowing motion of octopus and*
> *jellyfish under the sweep of a submarine current. There is*
> *a similar correlation of the elegant and decorative people*
> *with the clear-cut, extravagant vegetation; of their simple*
> *and sensitive temperament with the fertile land.*

The Balinese love nature and prefer to be in an architecture of grand outdoor spaces. They gather in *bale* that are open to warm breezes, natural light and vistas of lush tropical foliage. All the open spaces—compounds, temples and village streets—are their living spaces.

The author with a painting by I. Ketut Karja of Penestanan depicting a *gebogan agung* offering.

Tjilis The *tjili* motif represents Dewi Sri, the honoured rice goddess, and is often rendered in the shape of a woman. It assumes an hourglass shape formed by joining two triangles at their apex. In a three-dimensional representation, *tjilis* would have rounded breasts, long thin arms, large earplugs (earrings) and a fan-shaped crown as a head-dress. Frequently, the motif is abstract and perhaps never more beautifully executed than in the high offerings for temple ceremonies. These offerings, called *gebogan agung*, can be as tall as 3 metres and are fashioned on a stand with a cloth skirt. The body would be composed of fruits or vegetables; rice cakes or flowers would form the face; and the crown would be made of palm leaves.

TOP LEFT This entry gate has a stepped and rhythmic design above its door. The rooster and hen on the roof, as well as the curved wing-walls, add a touch of whimsy. Wall is made of coral-rock, enhanced with a paint stain to achieve a more brilliant colour.

MIDDLE Garden pathways, like these at Hotel Tugu Bali, are part of the outdoor architecture language of Bali.

TOP RIGHT Old Chinese ceramic stone tiles provide ventilation in this *paras taro* wall. *Paras taro* is a natural clay material embedded with small pebbles. Framing the tiles is a border of carved *paras krobokan*, a hard grey stone from Krobokan village. This stone is also used in the carved, horizontal designs at the top of the wall; its stepped, rhythmic pattern is one that is often seen in Balinese architecture and in the terraced rice fields.

BOTTOM A gate with faded glory, probably pre-Majapahit, leading into the palace at Tegalalang. Note the horizontal and vertical details of the gate, which repeat a stepped theme.

MATERIALS AND METHODS

For all its mass, a tree is a remarkably delicate thing. All of its internal life exists within three paper-thin layers of tissue—the phloem, xylem, and cambium—just beneath the bark, which together form a moist sleeve around the dead heart—wood. However tall it grows, a tree is just a few pounds of living cells thinly spread between roots and leaves. These three diligent layers of cells perform all the intricate science and engineering needed to keep a tree alive, and the efficiency with which they do it is one of the wonders of life. Without noise or fuss, every tree in a forest lifts massive volumes of water— several hundred gallons in the case of a large tree on a hot day—from its roots to its leaves, where it is returned to the atmosphere. Imagine the din and commotion, the clutter of machinery that would be needed for a fire department to raise a similar volume of water.

— *Bill Bryson,* A Walk in the Woods

ABOVE This coral-rock hill at Jembrana is being quarried. The stone will be used as a building material as well as a base for the construction of roads.

LEFT TOP & BOTTOM Workers at the woodworking factory of Made Sudiana Bendesa show deep respect for wood. Here, a treasury of ebony wood is carefully catalogued. The factory makes dining tables from thick slabs of mango, teak, *merbau*, hibiscus and jackfruit wood. A unique feature of the tables is that the bark is usually left intact, an organic textural reminder of the intricate nature of trees.

There is an abundance of exotic woods and hardwoods in Indonesia and all are within close proximity to Bali. The variety of timber is extensive and include mahogany, teak, jackfruit, coconut palm, bamboo, *merbau* and *bengkerai*; each has its own strength, colour and texture, which makes it a dream come true for designers who work with wood.

The ready availability of timber products has encouraged present-day architectural designers to consider the use of wood as a first priority when choosing materials for new structures. Furthermore, timber is part of the tradition of architecture in Bali and today's designers are continuing that tradition. They are also bringing other natural materials into the mix such as the wide variety of quarried stones from many different islands. Contemporary designers are creating a new architecture; although the emphasis is still on organic materials and using traditional elements of Balinese structures, what is new and has lifted the art of architecture to new levels is the way those materials have been combined and arranged.

Bali's interior was once lush with timber forests but these were depleted long ago. To meet the island's need for wood, the people turned to bamboo. Fortunately, bamboo grows naturally in the damp, shady and steep terrain of river ravines and the geography of the island has provided many ravines, a perfect answer to a small island's need to maximize land use for the cultivation of rice. How perfect the commensalisms of the living nature of being. Bamboo grows abundantly in the ravines, like a weed, in areas where rice cultivation is not possible and fits so many needs of the Balinese in its inherent qualities of strength, flexibility, fast growth as well as being light in weight.

Bamboo is a remarkable plant; it is actually a grass and can grow as much as one metre per day. Large posts and beams of bamboo make a handsome, organic material and are used in both residential and commercial structures. Large diameter bamboo, called *petung*, has the tensile strength of steel, yet is lightweight and can be harvested and delivered without the need for heavy equipment. Since accessibility to bamboo groves is often only by footpaths, a common sight on Bali is to see a large bamboo pole being transported from grove to construction site on the shoulder of a Balinese man. Until the last part of the 20th century, there were no power tools or automated equipment. Bamboo was not only available, it was easy to manage from grove to destination and the material could be worked by hand. These attributes certainly account for the widespread use of bamboo.

The Balinese were also very inventive in how to use this one material in ways that answered so many needs. Single lengths of *petung* bamboo, for instance, are used as water pipes or drainage pipes or in modern furniture; when lashed together, they are used to make a bridge. Smaller diameter bamboo such as *ampel, santong* or *hyas* are split and woven into mats to form airy walls called *bedeg* or woven into rugs. Split bamboo is also used as a material for roofing shingles in the drier, more northern parts of Bali (in the more rainy south, *alang-alang* thatching is found to be more durable). Village markets are full of products made from bamboo. There are baskets of all shapes and sizes to fit different practical needs; there are hats, umbrellas, toys, tools, utensils and musical instruments. If ever there was a need for a receptacle for work or storage or play, bamboo would have been the material of choice.

Bamboo is a quickly renewable resource with some species growing more than a metre per day. Being a lightweight material, it can be harvested by hand without the help of heavy equipment.

TOP LEFT Women harvest *alang-alang*, which will be tied to lengths of bamboo for use in making thatched roofs.

TOP RIGHT Workers sort and tie *alang-alang* to lengths of bamboo approximately 2 metres long to form shingles for roofs.

BOTTOM *Alang-alang* stacked in sheaves is ready to be made into roof shingles like those standing in the back, which will soon be delivered to a construction site.

OPPOSITE This is organic architecture, pure and simply perfect. This bamboo *pondok* has become a permanent residence: there is a verandah for the bicycle, bamboo blinds to keep rain out, and a trellis that used to be a tie-down for the thatch roof now supports a flowering vine. *Subak* water flowing by celebrates nature with tinkling water sounds.

THE CRAFTSMAN

Artistry is an integral part of life on Bali and evident in everyday, ordinary activities. In former times, the Balinese language did not include a word for 'art' or 'artist'. An artist was a craftsman with a particular skill that he used mainly in service to his religion. He did not receive money for work nor sign his name to his masterpieces. His labour was a gift. When European artists began to arrive on Bali in the 1930s, they brought with them a new way of thinking and looking at art. For the first time, the artisans of Bali began to view art for art's sake.

Contemporary Bali has since moved far along the path of art-for-sale. There is still, however, a recognition that craftsmen—whether woodcarver, stone carver, musician, painter, maker of exquisite offerings or weaver of fine fabrics—are merely working at the job at hand without an elevated concept of 'artist'. As Miguel Covarrubias wrote in *Island Of Bali* in the 1930s:

> *Unlike the individualistic art of the West in which the main concern of the artist is to develop his personality in order to create an easily recognizable style as the means to attain his ultimate goal—recognition and fame—the anonymous artistic production of the Balinese, like their entire life, is the expression of collective thought.*

Craftsmanship continues to flourish on Bali, with highly skilled individuals who have mastered their art through the traditions of their father and forefathers and who, in most cases, continue to work in a communal atmosphere. Villages are known for certain

LEFT Woodcarving shop of Made Sudiana Bendesa in Mas, Bali. Workers are carving complicated, three-dimensional panels that can be viewed from either the front or the back. These extraordinary panels are being carved for a temple in Japan.

ABOVE Without sketches or plans, chisel is taken in hand and inspiration guides the artist as he begins to carve the soft *paras* stone.

ABOVE Carved *paras* stone set in a wall of river stones at Spa Hati, a project of Bali Hati near Ubud.

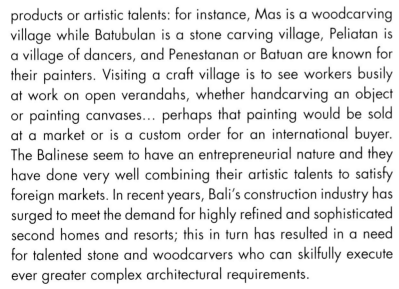

products or artistic talents: for instance, Mas is a woodcarving village while Batubulan is a stone carving village, Peliatan is a village of dancers, and Penestanan or Batuan are known for their painters. Visiting a craft village is to see workers busily at work on open verandahs, whether handcarving an object or painting canvases… perhaps that painting would be sold at a market or is a custom order for an international buyer. The Balinese seem to have an entrepreneurial nature and they have done very well combining their artistic talents to satisfy foreign markets. In recent years, Bali's construction industry has surged to meet the demand for highly refined and sophisticated second homes and resorts; this in turn has resulted in a need for talented stone and woodcarvers who can skilfully execute ever greater complex architectural requirements.

In Bali, stone and wood carvers are nearly always in demand because of the nature of the local and widely available *paras* stone. *Paras* is a soft, grey and ochre sandstone found in river

ravines. Being highly porous, it makes the perfect home for fast growing mosses and lichen and gives a highly desired aged appearance to even the most recently carved object. The combined effects of weather and plants on this soft stone means that it requires constant renewal. Therefore, it is not an unusual sight to see a stone carver busily at work in a temple, working away on the most elaborate designs to repair eroded stone. He uses neither drawings, measuring devices nor power tools. With only a chisel in hand, he begins to work on the complicated designs, in situ.

The same perpetual renewal, repair and replacement is required of wood structures and ornamentation as they are prone to damage by wood-boring insects and the ravages of a hot, humid climate. Woodcarvers work only with hammer and chisel; usually sitting on the floor with their feet holding on to a piece of wood, the chisel works away to produce intricately carved mouldings and sculptures.

The age of a building whether it be a temple or a village gathering pavilion is generally not known, and such information has little value to the Balinese. The importance of a building is not evaluated according to its age but only to its function or ancestral significance. Renovating and repairing such buildings is an age-old, ongoing duty of the village. It is communal commitment by the people to the past and to the future, honouring the principles of *adat*, *budaya* and *agama*.

The Balinese are proud of their traditions and honour their ancestral ways with an uninhibited spirit, yet they remain open to new ideas. Bali has felt the influence of many cultures, but the people have been able to adapt new concepts and translate them in a manner that is pure Balinese.

ABOVE This bathroom at Alam Indah Homestay in Nyuh Kuning was designed by Ketut Krinting. The carved designs on some of the stones of the wall and the use of an old stone water container as a sink gives this bathroom in a villa at his homestay a natural grotto feeling.

OPPOSITE Mythical figures carved in a block of dense Palimanan *paras* stone from Java.

Glossary

A

adat customary traditional cultural laws

agama religion

Agama-Hindu Bali name of the Balinese religion, which is a combination of Animism, Hinduism and Buddhism

alang-alang grass used especially for thatch roofs. Of the many kinds of grasses used, elephant grass is considered the most long lasting.

aling-aling wall just inside the entry gate to compounds and temples. The wall provides a screen from the street, but is also thought to ward off malevolent spirits since it is believed spirits have difficulty in making sharp turns. The wall also forms a momentary stop; just as the front door of western homes separates the outside world from life within the home, the wall serves to separate the outside world from life within the compound—even if the stop is only in the mind.

Arjuna one of the five Pandawa brothers, much loved heroes of the Hindu epic, the Mahabharata

B

bale traditional Balinese pavilion, built of wood, upon a raised platform; usually an open structure with a thatch roof

bale ageng pavilion in a palace reserved for rites of passage

bale agung literally means 'large bale'; often used for village events

bale dangin the honoured pavilion in a compound where rites of passage ceremonies and other important events in the life of the family are held. It is also the traditional *bale* for grandmothers and grandfathers to sleep.

bale meten sleeping pavilion for fathers and mothers. On the marriage of a couple's oldest son, the couple moves to another pavilion.

bale patok pavilion for viewing the landscape and socializing

banjar hamlet of a larger village with its own neighbourhood organization

banten an offering or tribute. All offerings are generically called *banten*. Each type of offering has a specific and defining name, for instance, ***canang*** is a type of *banten* with certain ingredients.

Barong a mythical, supernatural, benevolent creature seen as the mediator between good and evil in Balinese dance and drama. Every village has a sacred Barong costume brought out on special occasions and ceremonies. Similar to the Chinese lion, the Barong costume is treated with reverence, especially the face and head. Two men animate the costume—one manipulates the head and front legs while the other controls the body.

bata brick

batu stone

batu krobokan volcanic stone from the village of Krobokan

batu palimanan limestone of fine texture from the village of Palimanan in West Java

batu paras a soft, porous stone; volcanic tuff

bata bali generic term for all bricks; size and quality can vary

bata bola mud balls

bata citakan unfired mud bricks

bedeg woven lengths of bamboo forming a matting; commonly used as wall and ceiling materials in Balinese traditional architecture

bemo privately owned vans or small trucks with bench-style seating offering public transportation. *Bemos* can be flagged down along the roads; seating is often wedged between friendly Balinese, school children and baskets brimming with produce.

bengkerai hard wood that cracks or checks (small cracks) if used in sunny locations; a desirable choice of wood for exterior posts and beams

beringin tree banyan tree, also called *waringin*; symbolizes the family and is considered sacred

Bhagavad-Gita part of the Mahabharata Hindu epic

Boma (Bhoma) 'man-of-the forest', a benevolent demon with an awesomely fierce face; often seen above doorways

Brahman Hindu concept of a single, all pervading life-force, a totality of the universe

Brahma Hindu deity of fire

budaya customary cultural-civil law

bukit hill

C

canang small, everyday offering in a shallow tray of woven palm leaf; the offerings include fresh flower blossoms, a bit of cooked rice, sweet smelling grasses and a stick of incense

candi generally a dome-shaped Buddhist or Hindu shrine, often considered to be a memorial to royalty

candi bentar entry gate into the first courtyard of temples. The gate is split in two upright halves that are open at the top and is often likened to the image of hands formed in prayer.

canggahwang timber brace or bracket, part of roof structure of pavilions (canggah wang: tenon joint as in mortise and tenon)

capu manik sacred ceremonial bowl

cepuk rare and sacred textile of handspun coarse cotton or silk with a border of white arrowheads called *gigi* ***barong*** (*barong* teeth). The cloth has ***endek*** patterns with fine lines in the centre field using black, blue, yellow and white colours; background is always red or varying shades of red. A patterned border frames the cloth.

D

desa village

Dewi Sri the rice goddess

Dong Son drum kettledrum cast from metal, requiring no other implement or membrane to produce a sound. Kettledrums are idiophones, instruments made of a sonorous material like metal or wood that when struck will emit a sound. The gong of the ***gamelan*** orchestra is another example of an idiophone; when struck, it emits a deep reverberating sound.

E

endek the common textile in Bali; a weft **ikat** (only the weft threads are dyed before weaving)

G

Galungan the most important holiday in the Balinese Hindu cycle of ceremonies. It celebrates the victory of *dharma* over *adharma* (the ultimate law of all things over opposing forces).

gamelan Balinese orchestra

Garuda mythological bird-like eagle, the vehicle of Wisnu

gedong pasimpangan structure for honouring deities and storing temple heirlooms

geringsing double-**ikat** fabric made from cotton yarns in the village of Tenganan. Double-ikat fabrics are woven by dyeing both the weft and warp threads before weaving. The complexity of dyeing and weaving may require five or more years to complete a textile. Weavers from only two other places in the world produce a double-ikat textile similar to *geringsing*—Japan and India. Geringsing textile dyes result in muted colours of red to reddish-brown, dark blue and dark purplish-violet. Blood is used as a dye. Patterns and designs have triangles, animals, emblems and figures of the *wayang* (puppet) style. The woven cloth is considered to have magical power.

gong gede a musical group; also a large percussion instrument in the **gamelan** orchestra, usually made of bronze

gudang warehouse or shed for storage

Gunung Agung Bali's highest mountain (3,142 meters); considered 'the sacred mountain'

I

ibu mother or polite form to address an older woman

ijuk black fibre from the sugar-palm tree; used to make string or as thatching for roofs of shrines

ikat literally means 'to tie'. Ikat weaving is a time consuming, complicated process of dyeing and weaving fabrics. Before weaving, un-dyed threads are tied so that when the bundle is placed in dye, the tied portion does not take-up the dye and remain un-colored. Subsequent tying and dipping of the bundles of thread into dye creates patterns of intricate colourations. Either the weft threads or warp threads may be dyed. In the case of double-ikat, both weft and warp threads are dyed before weaving. The fabric obtained from the double-ikat method is called **geringsing**.

J

jalan road; jalan-jalan = walk; jalan kaki = footpath

joglo decorative centrepiece in a typical Javanese wooden house. Four solid posts support a carved ceiling beneath the main ceiling of a room. The ceiling of a *joglo* borrows its shape from the pagoda-shaped **meru** in that it has an uneven number of levels that diminish in size from bottom to top. Carvings on the ceiling are a blend of sacred Hindu motifs from India and the Majapahit era of Java.

K

kaja direction towards the mountain, **Gunung Agung**. If one lives south of the mountain, direction of *kaja* is to the north; if one lives north of Gunung Agung, then *kaja* means to the south, towards the mountain.

kamper rather soft wood commonly available and used throughout Bali

kangin East, or in the direction of the rising sun

karang murdha terracotta crown used as the final element on top of a roof; also helps divert rainwater away from the topmost point of a hip roof

karma belief that life is an endless cycle and that a person's actions in one state of existence will determine their fate in the next stage

kauh West, or in the direction of the setting sun

kelod direction towards the sea or directionally South. If one lives north of the mountain **Gunung Agung**, then *kelod* means to the north, away from the mountain.

kopi richly roasted Balinese coffee, ground to a powder. A measure is placed in cup to which hot boiling water is added.

kori gate

kori agung palace gate

kotatsu table low Japanese table where users sit on the floor and place their legs in an open space under the table. The table, which may be lowered into the opening to provide more floor space, is considered an emotional centre of a home, and one for family and friends to gather around.

kraton palace

kulkul hollow cylinder of bamboo or wood used as a signal drum

L

lamak coconut leaf mat usually woven in a long narrow strip and decorated with multi-coloured cut-outs; placed on shrines or objects as a special offering

lesehan act of sitting at low tables on floor cushions to dine

lingga (lingam) Phallic in shape, *lingam* is a symbol of Hindu God Siwa, the recycler of life. According to A. J. Kempers in *Monumental Bali*: "Taken together, the *lingga* and the **yoni** may be considered as symbols of Oneness, of the Totality of all phenomena in existence".

lontar book written on dried sugar-palm fronds. Archives of ancient *lontar* are studied for historical information relating to **adat**, **budaya** and **agama**.

losman homestay for tourists

lumbung rice granary

M

Majapahit refers to Javanese Majapahit Empire that migrated to Bali in the 14th century to escape autocratic rule of Islam on Java

mandi square, waterproof box (usually tiled) that holds water for the purpose of bathing; also means 'to bathe'

meru pagoda-shaped shrine, tiered with an uneven number of roofs

N

nawa sangga spiritual compass points; also known as **sangga mandala**

niskala the unseen world; the opposite is **sekala**, of this world

O

omong-omong to talk together

P

padmasana shrine placed in northeastern corner of temples; usually reserved for the sun god, Surya, or the Hindu trinity comprising Brahma, Siwa and Wishnu (see **trisakti**)

paduraksa main temple gate with roof

palebon cremation ceremony of royalty

palimanan stone quarried stone from the island of Java

paras taro hard clay stone with small stones embedded within from the village of Tegallalang

pasar market

pemangku village priest

penjor tall arching bamboo pole representing mountains

piasan pavilion in temples for offerings

poleng black- and white-checked cloth. White checks represent 'good' and black checks represent 'evil'. The balance of these forces is in the grey weave where the two colours are blended.

pondok small shelter, usually made from bamboo, built in rice fields for workers to rest

popolan adobe

pura temple

pura dalem temple of the dead or ancestors

pura desa town or village temple

pura pusih temple of origin

puri palace

purnama bulan full moon ceremony held on the first night of the full moon phase every month

S

sangga mandala spiritual compass points; also known as **nawa sangga**

saput small, flat cloth men tie over the sarong; usually bright yellow or white with a border of decorative trim sewn at the bottom

sawah wet-rice fields

sederhana simple or modest

sekala of this world; **niskala** being the unseen world

sendi column base, a bollard

subak organization village group that makes decisions on agricultural matters, especially in regard to irrigation of rice fields

T

tamu people from places other than Bali, outsiders

tjili decorative, abstract image of the rice goddess Dewi Sri

toko shop

tri angga three zones of spatial orientation—high, middle and low

tri hita karana the three causes of goodness

trisakti Hindu Holy Trinity, meaning three in one—Brahma, Siwa (Shiva) and Wishnu (Vishnu). Balinese believe in one god, Sanghyang Widi, as the supreme God in one. This supreme God has varying powers: as creator he is the God Brahma, as destroyer he is Siwa and as preserver he is Wishnu.

triwangsa the three privileged castes. The Brahmans are the priestly caste; Ksatriyas, the royal families; and Wesyas, the upper middle classes. The common people of Bali are called the Sudras. While the caste system established certain rules for the society, there was never a strict or unchangeable system.

trompong musical instrument in the gamelan orchestra

U

undagi Balinese priest-architect

W

wayang puppet

wayang kulit shadow puppet made from leather; dramas playing out the beloved Mahabharata

warung small food stand

wantilan large, open-air pavilion; social hall

Y

yoni symbolic of the vulva. **Lingga**-yoni symbolism is not thought of as male-female but of the triad—Siwa, Brahma and Wishnu.

yoshizu yoshi is a strong reed that grows on river banks. In Japan, it is used in houses of common people as an insert in doors and cabinets, for blinds or folding screens and especially in the summer season. It was popular in the Edo era (before 1868). The use of yoshi has all but disappeared in Japan. Today it is mostly seen in up-scale Japanese restaurants, tea rooms for the tea ceremony or in temples.

Architectural
notebook

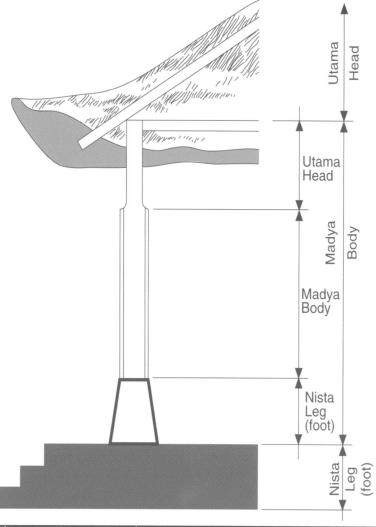

PRINCIPLES OF BALINESE ARCHITECTURAL DESIGN

The philosophy of TRI LOKA or TRI ANGGA explains the hierarchy of space and designates the physical world into three zones. The people of Bali are among the few island people of the world who turn towards the mountains rather than to the sea. It is believed gods and goddesses inhabit the mountains and other spirits (not necessarily evil) are in the ocean depths. The people live between the sea and mountains and must placate or strike a balance between these opposing forces.

Tri Loka (Three Places)	Swah Loka (Atmosphere)	Bhuwah Loka (Lithosphere)	Bhur Loka (Hydrosphere)
Tri Angga (Three Zones)	Utama Highest/Head	Madya Middle/Body	Nista Low/Foot
1 Universe	Atmosphere	Lithosphere	Hydrosphere
2. World/earth	Mountain	Land	Sea
3. Village	Temple	Community	Cemetery
4. Temple	Meru courtyard	Middle courtyard	Outer area
5. Compounds	Household shrines	Working and sleeping pavilions	Entry gate

The principles of Balinese architectural design include:

1. TRI LOKA, TRI ANGGA, spatial orientation
2. SANGA MANDALA/NAWA SANGGA, spiritual axis
3. MANIK RING CUCUPU — balanced cosmology. Architectural concept is a balanced integration of man, nature and god.
4. Human scale and proportion
5. Open-air pavilions, court concept
6. Truth of construction and materials

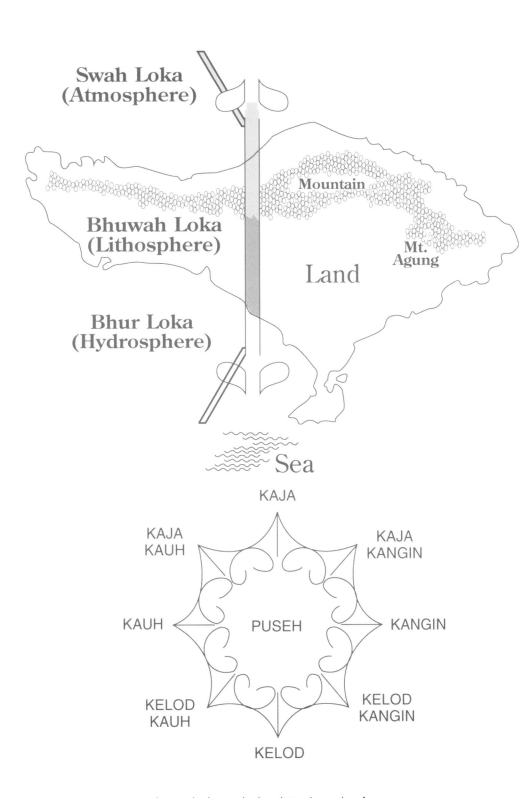

Structures relate to the human body utilizing hierarchy of space concepts.
Buildings are considered living organisms having a head, body and foot.

Sanga Mandala

The philosophy of spatial orientation, Tri Angga, is further complicated with the concepts of spiritual compass points called SANGA MANDALA or NAWA SANGA. Cosmological orientation consists of eight cardinal directions plus one centre point or focal point. Each of the nine cardinal directions have corresponding colours and deities.

Orientation to the great mountain, Gunung Agung, is central in Balinese life even in the most mundane of situations. The people must sleep with their heads towards the mountain or to the rising sun. It is believed the feet are an unclean part of the body and to point them towards the holy mountain would be unthinkable.

Puseh	Centre – multi-colour – deity Siwa
Kaja	North, towards the mountain – black – deity Wisnu
Kaja Kangin	Northeast – blue – deity Sambu
Kangin	East – white – deity Iswara
Kelod Kangin	Southeast – violet – deity Mahasora
Kelod	South, towards the sea – red – deity Brahma
Kelod Kauh	Southwest – orange – deity Rudra
Kauh	West – yellow – deity Mahadewa
Kaja Kauh	Northwest – green – deity Sangkara

The most influential axes are KAJA-KELOD (mountain-sea) and KANGIN-KAUH (sunrise-sunset). Orientation to spiritual axes rather than directional compass points of north, south, east and west further emphasize the Balinese concept of Bali as a microcosm of the Universe and the great mountain as the "navel of the world".

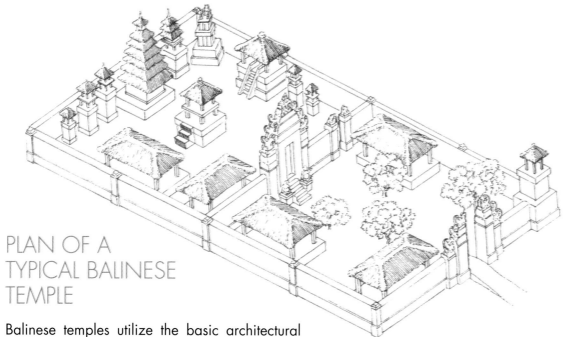

PLAN OF A TYPICAL BALINESE TEMPLE

Balinese temples utilize the basic architectural concept of open courtyards with various pavilions and shrines scattered about that allow for places to gather. Temples are enclosed by a low wall pierced with formal entry gates. This plan depicts two sacred courtyard areas. The outer area is usually defined by a large *beringin* (banyan) tree, revered as a symbol of the family.

A. **Candi Bentar** split-gate
B. **Kulkul tower** village signal drum
C. **Paon** kitchen for preparing feasts
D. **Bale Gong** pavilion for gamelan orchestra
E. **Bale** pavilion for resting or making offerings
F. **Paduraksa** ceremonial gate into most sacred area
G. **Gate** for worshippers to enter
H. **Aling-aling** stone wall (behind Paduraksa)
I. **Paruman** seat for gods
J. **Bale Piasan** pavilion for offerings
K. **Gedong Pasimpangan** place to store heirlooms
L. **Padmasana** stone seat for sun god, Surya
M. **Meru** pagoda-shaped shrine

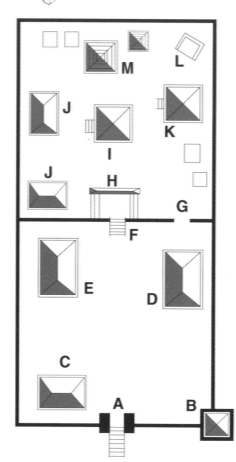

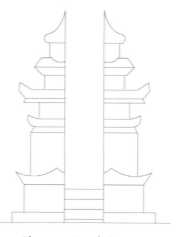

Elevation Candi Bentar

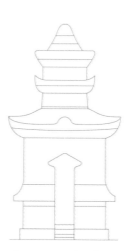

Elevation Paduraksa

Cross section of Meru

PLAN OF A TYPICAL BALINESE COMPOUND

Typical Balinese compounds exemplify open-courtyard planning that provides garden area for social gatherings. Several pavilions are enclosed by a wall. Social or economic conditions have little influence on the general layout of buildings within a compound. Rules of spatial organization according to cosmological orientation apply to everyone. Craftsmanship and quality of materials used are the variables seen in the homes of people of means and, of course, in palaces. However, even palaces adhere to the rules of balanced cosmology and spatial orientation.

A. **Aling-aling** wall
B. **Bale Tiang Sanga** social pavilion
C. **Uma meten** sleeping quarters and place for family heirlooms
D. **Sanggah Kemulan** family temple
E. **Bale Sikepat/Bale Sekenam** pavilions for sleeping or the making of offerings (4- and 6- post pavilion respectively)
F. **Paon** kitchen
G. **Lumbung** rice granary
H. **Tongos nebuk padi** cleared area for threshing rice

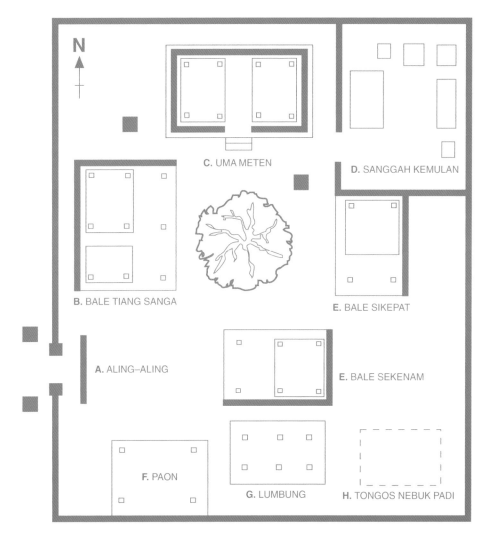

THE BALE

Schematic View of Traditional Construction Details

Bale are gathering places. A well-built *bale* is a masterpiece of design and construction. The materials used are indigenous to Bali, the structural technique is not labour intensive and the all-purpose room is open to the beautiful natural landscape as well as cooling breezes. This section drawing is of a typical *bale*. Traditional *bale* are built above the ground, are open on four sides with either four, six, nine or twelve coconut or bamboo posts. The structure is covered with *alang-alang* thatching and bamboo or wood rafters. The raised platform floor is built approximately 35 to 45 centimetres above the ground to provide a comfortable seating height.

Organic materials and structural details are exposed, revealing natural textures and colours. *Alang-alang* grass is sewn to ribs of coconut fronds or bamboo to form shingles which are then lashed to bamboo rafters using cord made from fibres of the sugar-palm tree. This handsome and practical roof is supported by posts and beams of carved wood or coconut tree trunks which are tied structurally by either tongue and groove technique or mortise and tenon.

KARANG MURDHA

The motif Karang Murdha resembles a crown and is placed at the centre top point of hip roofs, a hat for the 'head' of the building jauntily worn for adornment although there is a practical function as well. Decorative crowns drain rainwater, preventing water from penetrating into the *alang-alang* grass roof. Often made from terracotta, such crowns are also carved from wood or stone.

LUMBUNG

The *lumbung*, or rice granary, is a classic form of traditional architecture of Bali. Steeply sloping arched roofs help drain as much rainwater as possible. The rice storage area, built well above the ground, further protects the grain from moisture and rodents. The space beneath the storage area is put to good use with the construction of a platform about 40 centimetres above the ground. Here, all manner of things are stored or in some compounds, this space is used primarily by men on a rainy day as a gathering place to socialize. Structural posts are placed on concrete *sendi* to protect the wood from ground moisture and insects. The *lumbung* has been adapted for other types of structures, including homes mainly used by tourists.

BALINESE DECORATIVE ART

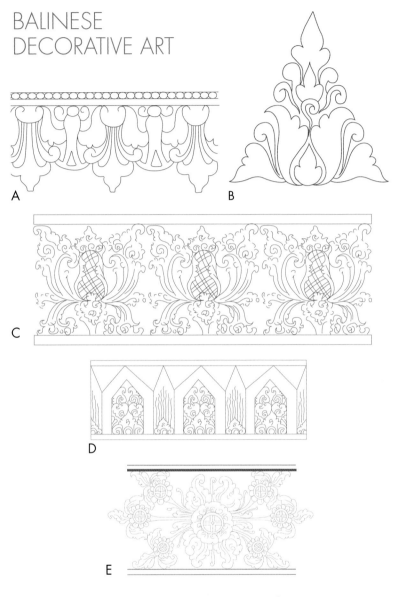

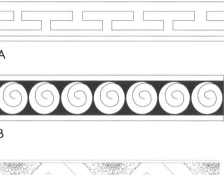

Floral designs accredited to Majapahit influence are widely used in stone and wood carvings, and can be found on statues, entry gates and walls or anywhere a decorative motif might be considered. Motifs are specific in combinations of vines, flowers and symbols; however there are always variations from one district to another or according to the whim of the artist.

A. **Patera Ring-ring**
B. **Patera Mas-Masan**
C. **Patera Sari**
D. **Patera Watu Allang**
E. **Patera Cina**

Here are further examples of decorative art used everywhere in Bali. Motifs A, B and C are some favourites in decorating walls or entry gates and may be worked with brick or carved on stone. Drawings of vines and tendrils, as in motif D, are a visual interpretation of foliage but also depict philosophic concepts relating human life to nature. Depicted within this motif is the nucleus of life as represented by the uncurling of a germinating seed (see shaded area). The Balinese sense of humour is seldom absent and makes itself known in this lovely design. Within the dotted box (right) is a design known as Kuping Guling—the ear of a pig.

A. **Motif Kuta Mesir**
B. **Motif Kakul**
C. **Motif Kuta Mesir Swastika**
D. **Motif Sambung**

A. **Patera Samblung** (border design)

Old Hindu Javanese decorative art seems to be a basis for much of the head motifs. Menacing faces dissolve into voluptuous floral motifs, certainly a case in point regarding contrasts and contradictions within Balinese art forms.

B. **Karang Tapel** (left), connecting piece **Ring-ring** and **Karang Goak** (right)
C. **Karang Daun Punggalan**
D. **Patera Punggal Majapahit**
E. **Karang Bunga**
F. **Karang Goak**
G. **Karang Asti Gajah**
H. **Karang Pakis**

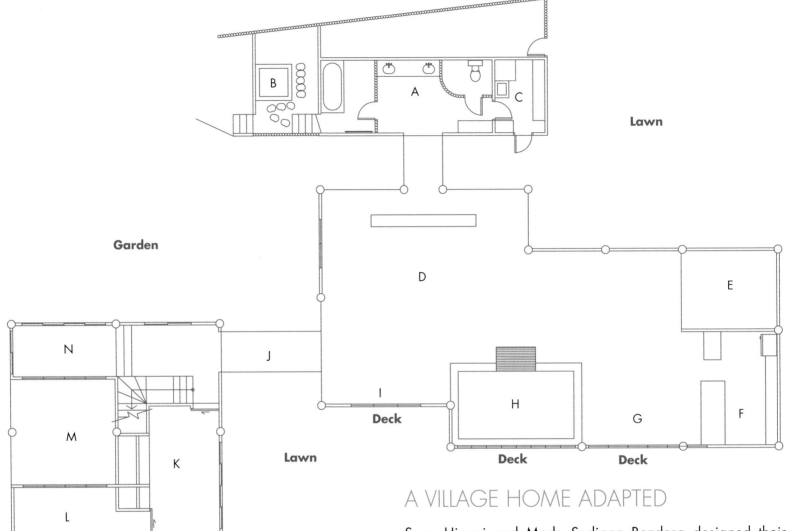

Lawn

Garden

Lawn

Deck

Deck   Deck

A. **Guestroom**
B. **Outdoor shower, mandi**
C. **Storage area**
D. **Dining, entertainment**
E. **Entry**
F. **Kitchen**
G. **Dining**
H. *Joglo*
I. **Sliding door**

J. **Steps to family pavilion**
K. **Library**
L. **Playroom**
M. **Children's study**
N. **Children's bedroom**

A VILLAGE HOME ADAPTED

Sana Hiromi and Made Sudiana Bendesa designed their home to provide plenty of space in the main pavilion for entertaining their many friends and business acquaintances. The first floor of the separate, two-storey pavilion is for family gatherings. Here their children have space to study and play near their bedroom, which was especially sized for tatami mats. On the entire second floor of this pavilion is a spacious master bedroom, a bathroom with a wooden Japanese soaking tub and a separate study room. Careful site planning takes full advantage of the expansive *sawah* landscape with views that gradually descend towards the Indian Ocean.

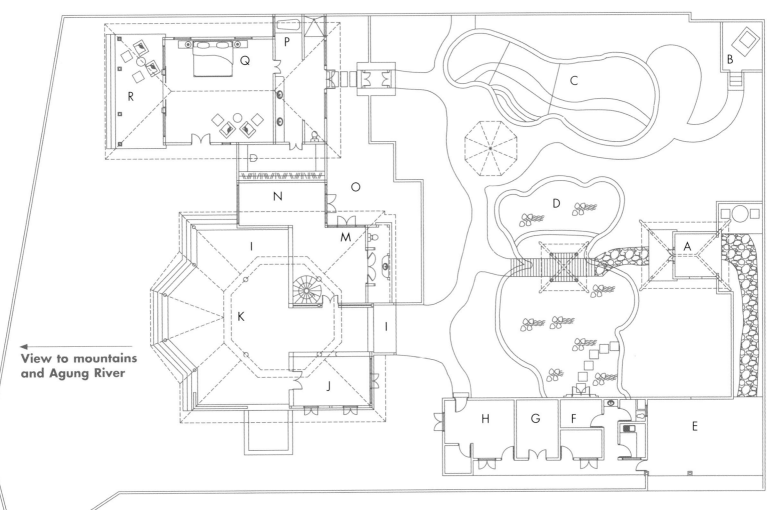

View to mountains and Agung River

A. **Entry gate**
B. **Family temple**
C. **Swimming pool**
D. **Lotus pond**
E. **Garage**
F. **Staff rooms**
G. **Store**
H. **Kitchen**
I. **Main entry**

J. **Pamela's room**
K. **Living room**
L. **Dining**
M. **Video room**
N. **Library**
O. **Garden**
P. **Bathroom**
Q. **Master bedroom**
R. **Terrace**

PURI NAGA TOYA

Puri Naga Toya, home of Pamela and Royal Rowe, is a well-composed work of art. Its three pavilions are planned around natural geographical features. The main living/dining/library pavilion on the first floor and a guest bedroom on the second floor have spectacular views to the mountains. Access to the guest bedroom is by the circular stairs in the library and video room. A second pavilion contains the master bedroom and bath, also with views of the mountains and river ravine. The staff rooms, kitchen and garage are located in a third pavilion near the access road and positioned to greet guests. Surrounding the three main pavilions and the entry gate pavilion are gardens and water features. *Bale* for animals, horse paddock and the *bale meten* guest cottage are not shown in this view.

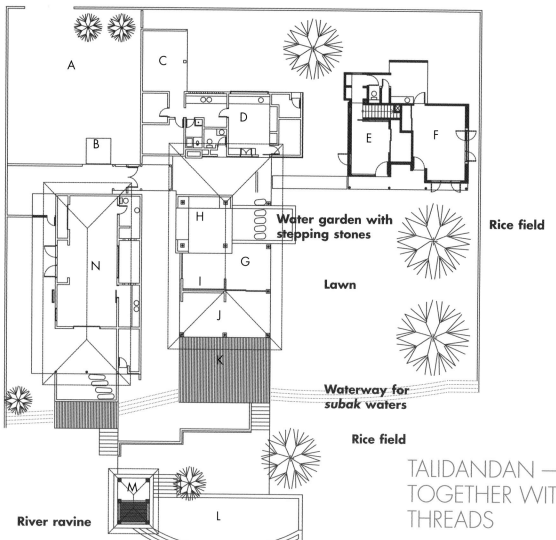

River ravine

A

C

B

D

E

F

Water garden with stepping stones

Rice field

H

G

Lawn

I

J

K

Waterway for *subak* waters

Rice field

N

River ravine

M

L

A. **Car court**
B. **Entry**
C. **Staff quarters**
D. **Kitchen**
E. **Office**
F. **Guest bedroom**
G. **Dining**
H. **Living room**
I. **Art niche on both sides of wall**

J. **Verandah**
K. **Deck**
L. **Swimming pool**
M. *Bale* **with spa pool**
N. **Guest wing**

TALIDANDAN — WALKING TOGETHER WITH SACRED THREADS

Talidandan is compact, yet expansive as each of the rooms open to broad views of rice fields and a river ravine. This home works well for entertaining or for guests staying awhile. The guest wing is a self-contained en suite pavilion with a small kitchen. The office and guest bedroom and bath are located in a separate pavilion connected to the kitchen and living areas by a garden walkway. The master bedroom suite takes up the entire second floor of this pavilion. The *subak* waters flowing through the property could have been a constraint in the design and site plan, as the stream may not be disrupted. However the waterway was used as an effective landscape element. The architect for this project was Joost van Grieken.

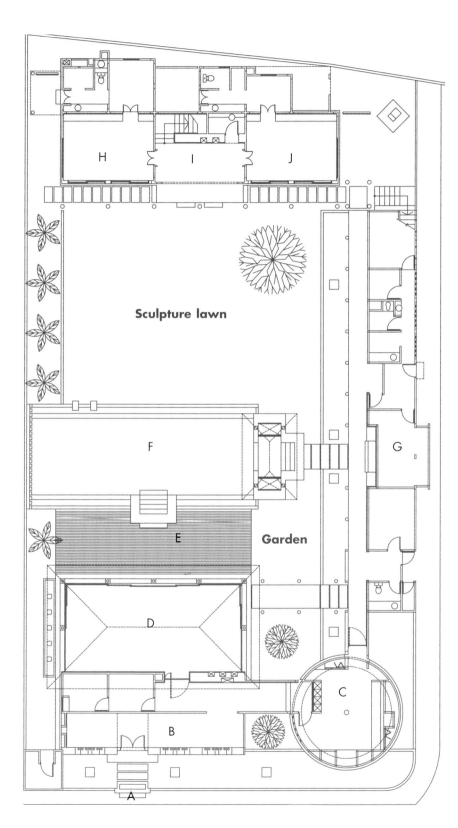

Sculpture lawn

F

E   Garden

D

C

B

A

H   I   J

G

VILLA RAMADEWA

Villa Ramadewa's owner Anthony Harrison and architect Joost van Grieken worked together to develop a modern approach to conventional Balinese design. The floor plan answers Tony's wish for open gathering places where friends and business acquaintances could come together in comfortable yet stylish spaces. Galleries and wall units were planned to display his growing collection of Southeast Asian art. The kitchen had to be of a scale that would cater to large dinner parties but often, according to Tony, it was "where on most occasions we all end up in the kitchen drinking wine whilst cooking". The master bedroom with a generous bath and dressing area, an open verandah and office/study room take up the entire second floor over the guest bedrooms. Above the staff quarters are a rooftop garden and sunbathing area. The urban plot of land is a deep and narrow site, yet the architect has successfully met the owner's design needs.

A. **Entry**
B. **Gallery for art**
C. **Kitchen**
D. **Living pavilion**
E. **Deck**
F. **Swimming pool**
G. **Staff quarters**
H. **Guest bedroom**
I. **Verandah for gathering**
J. **Guest bedroom**

Selected
bibliography

Bryson, Bill. *A Walk In The Woods*. Broadway Books, 1998.

Budihardjo, Eko. *Architectural Conservation in Bali*. Indonesia: Gadjah Mada University Press, 1990.

Coast, John. *Dancing Out of Bali*. Singapore: Periplus Editions, 2004. [Reprint]

Covarrubias, Miguel. *Island of Bali*. Hong Kong: Periplus Editions, 1999. [Reprint]

DeNeefe, Janet. *Fragrant Rice: A Tale of Passion, Marriage and Food*. Australia: HarperCollins, 2003.

Eiseman, Fred. *Bali Sekala & Niskala*. Hong Kong: Periplus Editions, 1990.

Goris, R. *Zie Bijdrage Tot Dekennis Der Oudjavaansche-En Balineesche Theologie*. Leiden, 1929. (Quote by Goris in Chapter 5 is also quoted in *Island Of Bali* by Miguel Covarrubias.)

Hobart, Angela, Urs Ramseyer and Albert Leeman. *The Peoples Of Bali*. Oxford: Blackwell Publishers, 1996.

Kempers, A. J. Bernet. *Monumental Bali: Introduction to Balinese Archeology & Guide to the Monuments*. Singapore: Periplus Editions, 1991.

Koke, Louise. *Our Hotel in Bali: How two young Americans made a dream come true: a story of the 1930s*. New Zealand: January Books, 1987

Leuras, Leonard. *Ubud is a Mood*. Bali: The Bali Purnati Centre for the Arts, 2004. Email: purnati@dps.centrin.net.id.

McPhee, Colin. *A House in Bali*. Hong Kong: Periplus Editions, 2000. [Reprint]

Pucci, Idanna. *The Epic of Life: the Balinese Journey of the Soul*. Nashville: Vanderbilt University, 1986.

Venturi, Robert. *Complexity and Contradiction in Architecture*. New York: Museum of Modern Art, 2002.

Vickers, Adrian. *Bali: a Paradise Created*. Australia: Penguin Books, 1989.

Walker, Barbara and Rio Helmi (photographs). *Bali Style*. Singapore: Times Editions, 1995.

Wijaya, Made (Michael White). *Architecture of Bali: A Source Book of Traditional and Modern Forms*. Latitude 20 Books, 2003